HOW TO BE A WINNER

Inside the Mind of a
Champion

Billy Schwer

How to be a Winner – Inside the Mind of a Champion

ISBN: 978-1-0682391-0-6

Published by Creative Words Ltd

First edition

First published in 2024

www.billyschwer.com

Editorial support and publication assistance from Creative Words Ltd

www.creativewords.cc

Mental Boxing™ is a registered trademark of Billy Schwer.

BILLY SCHWER

ABOUT THE AUTHOR

World Champion boxer, Billy Schwer had 137 fights on his journey to the top. He won multiple titles in his 20-year career – both amateur and professional – including British, Commonwealth, European and World Boxing Championships.

After retiring he embarked on a new journey and transformed into a professional speaker and personal performance coach. Trained by experts such as Werner Erhard, Eckhart Tolle, Dr Joe Dispenza and Gabor Maté, he uses boxing as a metaphor to teach resilience, courage and teamwork to individuals and organisations.

With advanced certifications in performance-based therapy coaching skills, Billy also volunteers as a Samaritan, assisting those in crisis.

Billy is on a mission to help business leaders and their teams to live a life full of passion, power and purpose and to help them win in every aspect of life.

WHY READ THIS BOOK?

For a little over twenty years I was a boxer, striving to get to the top. And, after 137 fights and a lot of setbacks, I made it. World Champion. Top of the World!

And then what? What do you do when the dream you've had since you were eleven comes true?

In the twenty-plus years since I first faced that question, I've come across countless people in the same position. They've set themselves a big goal and have either achieved it and now don't know what comes next or found that it was never going to happen for them and felt lost.

It took me a lot of self-examination and the facing of some hard truths to work out who I really was and what I wanted from my life. Now, though, I am living a life full of passion, power and purpose.

This book is for anyone who wants to live a ten out of ten life and is willing to put in the work to achieve it. I'll share with you the traits you need to be a winner. It won't be an easy ride – you will be facing the toughest opponent of them all: the mental boxing that is within you. But, if you step up into the boxing ring of life with a willingness to learn and take on the fight of your life, it will be worth it.

CONTENTS

INTRODUCTION

You can get it if you really want
But you must try, try and try, try and try
You'll succeed at last

Jimmy Cliff

My name's Billy Schwer and I'm a recovering boxer. What I do now to help my recovery and keep me winning is to inspire and empower people to live with passion, power and purpose.

Would you like to have more passion in your life?

Would you like to be more powerful?

Would you like to be living a life of purpose?

Then this book is for you.

I boxed, I competed and I fought 138 times, as an amateur and a professional boxer, 45 of them as a pro, winning the British, Commonwealth, European and the World Championship.

Now, through the pages of this book I'd like to share with you some of the winning traits that enabled me to do that. I promise you, if you apply these traits to yourself, your work and your life, you will win more often.

Would you like to win more often?

Would you like to experience more success?

Would you like to be able to punch above your weight in all that you do?

I have an invitation for you. I'd like to invite you to really engage in the pages of this book and be part of the experience, because that's where the magic is. If you look back over your life, the big lessons that you've learnt have probably come from the experiences you've had. They won't necessarily have come from what someone may have told you or from what you may have read.

I'm committed that when you finish reading this book, you'll be thinking and feeling differently about yourself, your life and your future.

I became a world boxing champion, a lifetime's work, in pursuit of a dream. I got to the top in what is arguably the toughest sport there is – professional boxing – then my life took a turn for the worse. I crashed and burned. In my first defence of the world title I got knocked out. I was carried out of the ring on a stretcher and put into the back of an ambulance. There I was on the way to hospital, sirens blaring as we dodged through the traffic. I was conscious but I was uncertain of my future health. I was frightened. I'd stepped up into the ring that night as I always did, prepared to die and maybe I was about to …

Professional boxing is a beautiful, brutal business. That night in hospital, I realised that my life as I knew it, was over. I made the toughest decision I've ever made: to retire from the professional boxing ring.

Have you ever made a life changing decision? If not, you will have to at some point.

If you know you need to make one right now and you haven't, what's stopping you?

My whole world fell apart and I went through an identity crisis. All my life I'd been Billy the Boxer. Suddenly, I was just Billy.

Who is Billy? Who am I? What am I doing? Why am I doing it? What does it all mean?

That's when I put these two words together *Mental* and *Boxing*. I was in a mental boxing match with that annoying voice in my head. You know the one – it never shuts up. If you're thinking, "What voice?" – that's the one!

Do you ever find yourself doing that – talking to yourself? Beating yourself up?

Life was pushing back, I was up against the ropes, I dropped my guard and the impact was devastating. I wrecked my marriage, ending up in divorce. I went bankrupt and my home was repossessed, I had no money and no future. Everything I'd fought so long and hard for was now gone. I felt like a failure.

I hit rock bottom and spiralled into depression, mentally breaking down and having suicidal thoughts. Some nights I'd go to bed not wanting to wake up.

Twenty-plus years ago when I retired from boxing, mental health wasn't openly discussed like it is today. I was trapped in a mental hell, embarrassed, ashamed and too proud to ask for help. My training and conditioning as a boxer taught me how to fight, defend, resist, confront and attack. Asking for help seemed like a weakness. But I learnt the hard way that true strength lies in vulnerability and seeking support.

Athletes have coaches, businesspeople have coaches and sometimes, we need a coach for our lives, so I got myself one.

I realised that what had me be a champion in the ring, being aggressive, domineering, overpowering, selfish, inconsiderate, always being right… was now seeing me fail in life (ask my ex-wife, she'll tell you). I just didn't know how to BE anything other than Billy the Boxer. I started to peel back all the layers of my identity to discover who Billy really was. And what a journey! It wasn't pretty. It was painful at times, I faced my truth, and my ego didn't like it one bit. It got well and truly beaten up.

I wanted to be free. Free from the constraints 'the boxer' had imposed upon me. I wanted to reinvent and recreate myself. What I realised as I was going through my crisis was that for some of us to wake up, we need a wakeup call. I certainly got mine!

I started reading, listening, studying and attending seminars. I went on seminar after seminar after seminar… I became a seminar junkie! I loved it.

And that's the journey I've been on for over 20 years now. The funny thing was, as I was working on myself, I started to learn how to coach, mentor and train others. It was then that I realised how much I love people, which shocked me because I'd spent all my life bashing people up (or getting bashed up, more like). I awakened to my life's purpose: to inspire and empower people to live with passion, power and purpose.

I do that through public speaking, writing and coaching. I speak at big conferences and go into companies of all sizes to share my expertise in personal performance. I consult and advise entrepreneurs, company owners, leaders and their teams. I use a mix of therapy-based performance coaching methods. I work one-to-one and with groups. I also volunteer for the Samaritans, a charity aimed at the prevention of suicide. I'm what they call a listener…

All these things have led me to feeling happier, more fulfilled and satisfied than I've ever been. I'm experiencing life as a ten out of ten.

And that is what I wish for you…

Winning doesn't mean someone has to lose

Before we get stuck in, I wanted to make something clear. When I talk about winning, I don't mean the kind of winning where you are beating your opponent to the punch and approaching everything with a 'kill or be killed' attitude. That works if you are a boxer but this is the real world.

The winning I'm offering you here is the type of winning that you could only imagine having; the life where your relationships are fulfilling and balanced; where your work gives you joy and satisfaction; where you invest time in yourself and for yourself to give you great life experiences; where everyone around you gains from your presence.

How that looks and feels will be different for every person who reads this book. My aim is to help you get clear on what winning means for you and then apply the traits within these pages to look, feel and experience that success.

Seven traits to be a winner

Reaching our full potential comes from recognising, exploring and studying the daily mental boxing match we have with ourselves and seeing how this can sometimes limit us. Through the pages of this book, I'll be sharing the seven traits you need to be a winner in your life. They are

- Be Aware of The Choices You're Making – Win or Lose You Choose

- Have The Courage to Take a Risk – KO Fear

- Never Give Up – Fight for What You Want

- Focus On the Future, Not the Past – Roll with the Punches

- Be Resilient in All Areas of Your Life – Take It on the Chin

- Be Willing to Look at Things Differently – Jab and Move

- Be Responsible for Who You Are – Own Your Life – BoxClever.

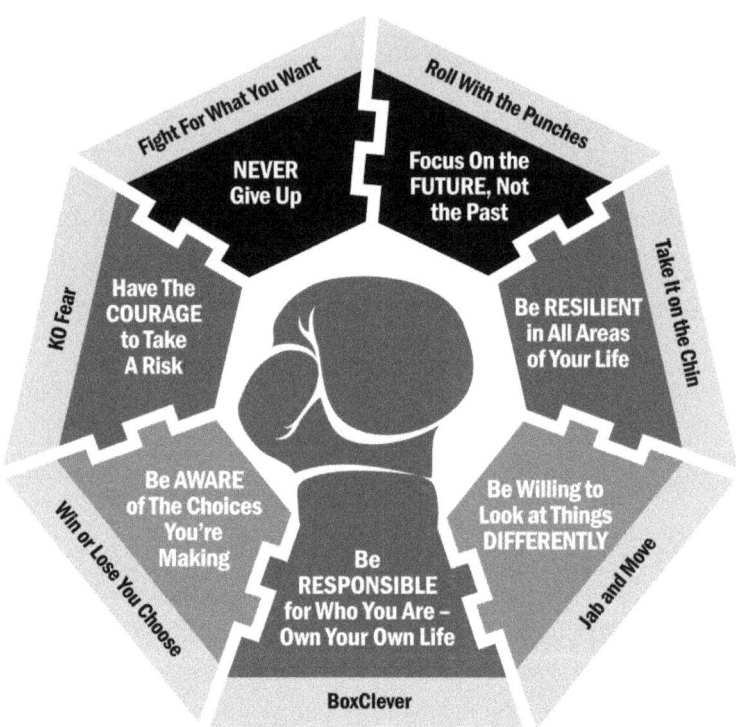

The most important thing to remember about these traits is that they aren't in any particular order and they all interconnect. At any moment in your life you might need to apply two, three or more of these traits to give you the clarity and direction you need.

How to get the most out of this book

I don't know about you, but I'm not a great fan of books that need an instruction manual to read them. That said, I did want to explain how I've set this book out so you can make the most of it.

INTRODUCTION

I do recommend that you read it with an open mind. I'm setting out seven traits for being a winner and some of them might challenge your thinking. So, approach each one willing to learn something new and to have an experience as you explore a new way of operating and looking at life.

I've written each chapter out to a set format. For each trait I will:

- Explain the trait and what it means

- Illustrate how I first recognised that trait in my journey to the World Boxing Championship and beyond

- Give you the 'punch line' – a short version of the trait which is easy to remember – and explain how you can apply this trait in your life

- Share wisdom from one (or more) of my teachers in life and how it relates to this trait

- Use case studies of historical figures and people I've met during my life to show how the trait shows up

- Point out the downsides of the trait if you take it too far or fail to balance it out with other winning traits

- Provide three exercises to help you explore the trait further for yourself

- Summarise the whole chapter as a recap and so you can revisit it for a reminder should you need it (And, let's face it, for those of you who are pushed for time and just want the summarised version).

Stop and Think

As you go through each trait, you'll notice boxes like these. They are designed for you to take a moment and reflect on your own experiences in life so you can start to see how the trait applies to you.

As you read, I invite you to take notes. By all means scribble on the pages as you go along or get a notebook. I've also created a worksheet which summarises each trait, provides space for you to write your own reflections and complete the exercises.

More important than anything else – go for it! If you want to be a winner in your life, the first step is always to take action.

Let's get it on!

BoxClever with Billy

Download the worksheets via this QR code

HOW TO BE A WINNER

BE AWARE OF THE CHOICES YOU ARE MAKING

"Your life is a result of the choices you have made. If you don't like your life, start making better choices.

Zig Ziglar

Do you ever feel like you have no choice? That we can't control anything and life is just 'the way it is?'

We all feel that way sometimes but think about it for a moment – feeling that way is a choice in itself.

You can choose.

Would you like being the cause of your life and not at the effect of it? Because, if you let life happen to you instead of going out and happening to life, you become the victim. You are settling for a life where opportunities pass you by and, despite every goal you hit, you still feel like a loser.

This crucial first trait of being a winner – in your life, your work, your relationships, everything in fact – shapes everything else we are working toward together through this book.

You made a choice in reading this far. You made a choice whether to read or listen on audio. You made a choice whether to commit to the exercises at the end of each chapter or just read the words and see what sticks.

Everything we do is a choice. Scientists think we make around 35,000 choices every day. That's a lot of choosing!

Quite a lot of those choices, of course, are unconscious. Choosing to get up, what to wear, what to eat, which route to take to work … Some are so automatic we don't even notice we are making them.

And that's what can knock you out! If you don't make conscious choices, you'll be making unconscious ones – operating on autopilot and doing the same things over and over again.

Many of the choices we make come from past learning. Maybe you have a Sunday Roast each week because that was what you did as a kid. Or you say a little poem to remember how to spell "difficulty" because you learned it at school[1]. All harmless stuff.

But what about the past learning that wasn't so helpful or comforting?

We can start forming an opinion about ourselves as early as two years old and, through our experiences as we grow into adulthood, we choose, consciously or unconsciously, who we are and build an identity around that. And that shapes everything we do and say and the goals we set ourselves in life. It shapes who we believe we are.

> **Stop and Think…**
>
> …about that for a moment. If the person you are today has come from the choices you made in the past, that means that **the choice you make today will shape your future.**

Why I became Billy the Boxer

There I am at five years of age, in my Mum and Dad's front room with my two older sisters: Lisa, who is eight, and Mandy who is eleven. We've been playing together, pretend-fighting and rolling about on the floor, as kids do. I am the youngest so of course they

---

[1] For the youngsters in the room, in the days before spell-checkers, we had to learn tricks to spell difficult words!

tease me and push me about. This day, they have me pinned on the floor. Mandy is holding my arms down, Lisa is sitting on my chest, and they are both leaning over me, sweeping their beautiful long blonde hair in my face. They're singing "Billy, Don't be a Hero" at me.[2]

I hated it – so, of course, they did it to me often. Anyone who has siblings will know how that goes!

I'm lying there on the floor, helpless. I'm kicking and screaming and struggling against them, but it is two against one and I am only little, so I can't fight them off. I get so angry and upset that I'm hyperventilating. It feels like I'm dying[3].

In that moment, I make an unconscious decision: "I can't fight my sisters off, so I must be weak."

From then on, I had to find a way to prove I wasn't weak. I was determined to prevent anyone from ever beating me up again. I needed to cover up the fact that I was weak and prove to the world that I could survive despite that. My sisters instilled a will to fight in me.

---

[2] A popular song at the time, by Paper Lace (we older people will know it – if you're a youngster, you can Google it).

[3] To be clear – they weren't torturing me and they had no idea it was causing me so much distress. Siblings do this, and to Mandy and Lisa it was just a game with their little brother.

The choices we make in the past (consciously or otherwise) impact our future.

For the next three years I struggled for survival. I was dyslexic with ADHD in an era when it wasn't understood or diagnosed (I was considered to be 'slow' or 'stupid') and avoided anything that would show me up to be weak. By the time I reached the age of eight I decided to be a boxer.

Fast forward three years and I'm 11 years old. I've taken up boxing with the Luton Boys Club, just around the corner from where we lived, and I'm competing in my third amateur boxing fight. It was at a black tie evening event for a gentlemen's club at the Dacorum Pavilion in Hemel Hempstead[4]. Everyone is smoking cigars, so the room is thick with it. And we're there, myself and Jason Meager from Berkhamsted Amateur Boxing Club, in a big arena, boxing for three rounds for their amusement.

And I lost! I was beaten on points.

I was devastated. I stood in the centre of the ring, in floods of tears, shattered at this defeat. My Dad, who was my coach, was trying to console me. And there, in that moment, I made another unconscious decision. I decided that I wasn't good enough.

---

[4] Now demolished to make way for The Forum council buildings

I'm 11 years old and believing that I'm weak and I'm not good enough. Those two choices meant I had to prove myself to the world.

Nothing less than being a world champion boxer would be enough.

Win or Lose, You Choose

Be the cause, not at the effect of your life. Choose how to respond and react to the situations and circumstances that surround you.

Of course, in the heat of a moment someone pushes your buttons, you get triggered and come out fighting. That's human nature. But, once the initial impulse has died off, you can choose to see your reactions and take a different path. Over time, with practice, you can even anticipate your reactions to certain situations and catch yourself before you lose it.

Stop and Think

Do you have a 'hot button'? Something that winds you right up, the moment you see or hear it. Something that, on reflection, isn't all that important? Maybe you go wild when someone doesn't indicate at roundabouts; perhaps you hate those annoying wheelie bags, which only seem to have been invented to trip you up; maybe that badly designed banking app which makes it impossible to just pay a bill without fifteen layers of authentication drives you nuts.

You'll have your own list. Choose one of them and make a point of noticing every time it pisses you off. Catch yourself and see how long it takes for you to come down off the ceiling. Choose to calm down and, over time, see whether it continues to trigger you in the same way every time.

You may have always thought that those hot buttons were just the way you were and you had no control over them but can you now see how you are not your thoughts? You actually have a choice. Those little hot buttons are a simple thing to practice on because, once you have learned that method of catching negative reactions, you can apply it to overcoming your limiting beliefs.

What do I mean by limiting beliefs? Any thought that holds you back in life. They are your Mental Boxing opponents.

They often start with a negative statement: I can't... I'm no good at... I'm not... Or they might describe you in a negative way: I'm weak... I'm ugly... I'm useless... These are the stories you are telling yourself about who you are. You've decided you are useless and then, guess what, you go looking for evidence that proves it. Just remember, they are only stories.

Practice spotting them and see how they are blocking you from a better future. Choose to parry their mean little jabs instead of letting them smash you in the face. Choose a better story for yourself.

Wisdom from my teachers in life

Throughout my life, I have learned a great deal from the wisdom of others. From my dad, who was my first coach, and all the others in my team who helped me become a world champion, through to the scholars, scientists, philosophers and coaches who have guided me through my transformation. There is always something to learn. I wouldn't be where I am today without them.

As we explore each trait of a winner, I want to share some of that wisdom with you. So, let's start with one of the masters in his field, Dr Joe Dispenza.

It was his book, *Breaking the Habit of Being Yourself* that first captured my attention. Dispenza is a chiropractor and a scholar of neuroscience. He has applied his expertise to quantum theory and how the power of the brain can create any reality.

Quantum theory is a complex concept spanning physics, chemistry, mechanics and more. The aspect of the theory that Dr Joe explores is that all possible outcomes exist. That can be a bit mind-boggling to grasp so, for a simple way to understand it, try watching *Sliding Doors*, starring Gwyneth Paltrow. You see two alternative lives unfold purely as a result of whether she catches a train or misses it.

In *Breaking the Habit of Being Yourself,* Dispenza explores the difference between thoughts (coming from the mind) and feelings (coming from the body) and how they interact to choose our reality. All versions of reality exist, waiting in the quantum field for us to connect with them and make them real.

The version of life where you are happy, fulfilled and satisfied is just as likely as the one where you are fed up, frustrated and discontented. You just have to choose which one you want and focus on it.

Simple in theory, but difficult in practice because 95% of what we do is habit. We don't even know we are making choices, let alone have control over them, until we go to work on what our mind is doing and start to notice the patterns.

What's more, we identify closely with our habits: "I'm shy", "I'm forgetful", "I'm chaotic" and the stereotypes (life's 'boxes') we put ourselves into or are put into by other people.

I have ADHD – it's a box I've put myself in. It would be very easy to use that as an excuse and a get-out clause for not living a ten out of ten life. After all, it is classified as a disability so surely that explains my belief of not being good enough. Because, according to the medical profession, I'm not.

I choose differently. I choose to accept that my brain works differently, ask for help when I need it and embrace the aspects of ADHD which are really powerful – such as an intense drive, immense creativity and massive resilience. I wouldn't bet against myself – there is nothing I cannot do!

Stereotypes block the brain and unconscious habits keep us trapped.

So, the more conscious you are about how you think, what you believe and how that influences your actions, the better chance you have of creating a new you and a new future.

That starts by knowing and accepting how you are now and how everything you have experienced in the past has shaped you. Then you can start to reprogramme your brain as you choose a different alternative.

Why do people make stupid choices?

Have you ever looked at a news headline and seen that someone in the public eye has landed themselves on the front page by doing something really stupid: Hugh Grant having "a moment of insanity" when he engaged the services of a prostitute and had sex with her in his car; Will Smith losing his rag at a poor joke made by Chris Rock and slapping him at the Oscars; whole bunches of politicians imposing a lockdown on the country and then throwing a party that broke all their own rules...

I've made some really stupid choices in my life. As a boxer my life was shaped by a mindset of 'kill or be killed' and taking risks. When I left boxing, that mentality really didn't work. My tendency to take risks meant that I made some bad investments and piled up debt on multiple credit cards. I went bankrupt. Not once, but twice!

Why on *earth* do people do things like that? And why on *earth* do we all make similar mistakes?

There are a number of reasons this happens – and it happens to us all.

1. **Overconfidence**. Sometimes we just get cocky and make a choice because we believe that it can't possibly go wrong. In 1995, Nick Leeson, a derivatives trader at Barings Bank, took risk after risk and, because early gambles made huge profits, kept on with a strategy even though it was no longer working. He covered up the losses and, in the end, bankrupted one of the oldest merchant banks in the UK.

2. **Decision fatigue**. Sometimes we are so drained by all the decisions we have made that we no longer have the mental capacity to make good choices. So, we either procrastinate (avoid choosing), take an easy route, or make a choice and then regret it (confusing everyone around you). How many decisions a day do you suppose you have to make if you're the President of the United States of America? Might that (at least partly) explain why Richard Nixon felt it was okay to spy on his

opposition and Bill Clinton choose to have an affair with his intern?

3. **Information Overload**. Sometimes there is so much information on hand that we can't see the wood for the trees. In a state of stress and confusion we might miss something vital. In January 1989, a Boeing 737 crashed onto the M1 motorway in Kegworth, Leicestershire. The left engine was malfunctioning but, because of smoke coming from the right side of the cabin, a change in the way the aircraft operated and unclear instructions from his co-pilot, the captain shut down the right (fully functioning) engine. Putting all the thrust into an already damaged engine, it caught fire and the plane came down 2 miles short of the East Midlands Airport.

4. **The 'What the Hell' effect**. Sometimes, life and circumstances have led us to a point where we decide we've already "blown it" so may as well do more of the same. Once we've made a first mistake or error in judgement, further poor choices no longer seem to matter. A simple example is when one is on a diet and then breaks it by eating a chocolate – then going on to empty the entire box. We've all done that!

When the choices make you

When I was a boxer, committed to becoming World Champion to show that I wasn't weak and I was good enough, I had a team around me and my life was set in a pattern. I had chosen to be World Champion and all other choices pointed in that direction. I was conditioned and trained and programmed to be a fighter. Fight, defend, resist, confront and attack. How I behaved was driven by the need to get to the top.

I was persistent and determined. I was tough and courageous. But I was also aggressive, domineering and inconsiderate. I was always right and completely selfish. The world revolved around Billy the Boxer.

Then, lying in the back of an ambulance, my career ended. I was no longer 'Billy the Boxer' but I knew of no other way to behave.

Everything I did and was, that worked beautifully in a boxing arena, didn't work in life. Some of the choices I made in the early years after my boxing career came to an end were pretty dubious. I made some really poor business decisions and chose to be in the wrong relationships. I cast about looking for a career that defined me (big learning here: it isn't the career that defines you – **you** define your career) and tried a range of different things.

I went back on the building site (I did an apprenticeship in my teens) but I was rubbish at it.

I was going to be a movie star and even did a few films. I'm proof that there **is** a 'worst actor ever!'

I was going to be a full-time personal trainer. It turns out that I can't do anything full-time with my ADHD.

I was going to be a photographer, so played around with that for a while but then gave it up.

I had a go at playing golf… nah!

I was going to open a wine bar and restaurant but I figured I'd just end up as the drunk at the end of the bar, drinking all the profits.

I had a go at being a courier driver. I just kept getting lost.

I thought about being a yoga teacher. I wasn't bendy enough.

I was going to get a job in the city as a trader, on the stock market. I decided that, with my background in boxing, I'd probably end up trying to knock someone out every time the market dipped.

I was going to be a boat skipper (I had visions of driving those big yachts around the south of France and the Bahamas). My training was on the North Sea, in the rain, in a rusty old boat. I spent most of my time throwing up over the side. That wasn't it.

I got involved with a nutritional supplement business.

I bought out a sportswear range.

I took up deep-sea diving and horse riding (not at the same time though).

I tried everything. I even had a go at modelling. I was with a modelling agency called *Uglies* who cater for people with unusual looking faces. I think Groucho Marx had me in mind when he said, "I never forget a face, but in your case, I'll be glad to make an exception!" I used to model balaclavas!

I wasn't any good at any of these things and nothing felt right. I was left feeling uncertain, unsure and unfulfilled, with only thoughts of, "This ain't it."

So, I had to unravel and unlearn all my conditioning and programming because it was based in the past and no longer worked for me. I persistently pursued my purpose with passion and power.

If all your choices have been pointing towards a specific, defined goal, make sure you know what you are going to do when you get there. Because when you get that top job, or smart car, or win the medal, the rest of your life is stretching out ahead of you and you don't have a plan. It's the difference between making choices towards something you want to *do* and making choices towards someone you want to *be*.

"I want to be World Boxing Champion" was a *do* choice. It drove me until I got there. I work with countless businesspeople – especially entrepreneurs, sales managers and leaders – driven by similar *do* goals who, having got there, realise their lives are a bit empty.

"I want to live a life of passion power and purpose" is a *be* choice. There is no end point – it is an ongoing practice of recognising and being aware of the choices you make.

If you have been *doing* instead of *being,* you might have to unlearn a few things and choose to give up a few things to create a new future for yourself. You'll need to find the traits that work for you.

When I retired from boxing, I had to choose a new future; and it was a challenge. I didn't feel the same as I had when I was Billy the Boxer. I didn't have the same kind of power that I had and I ended up being a victim.

It was only when I started to look at the choices that I was unconsciously making that I started to break free, to be myself and create the life I'm now living. And it took some doing.

WIN OR LOSE, YOU CHOOSE

Exercises

1. List some of the *do* goals you've had in life (things you've wanted to have, own or achieve). What happened when you achieved them? How did you feel afterwards?

2. Think back over your past. What limiting beliefs have you arrived at? List them and for each one, write about the things you've done in your life that prove otherwise.

3. What is the future you want to have? And what choices do you need to be making today to help that future come about? Who can you share this with?

Summary

This first trait of being a winner, is all about choices. We all make choices, all the time and every day, and many of them are unconscious, automatic and formed by the beliefs we hold about ourselves.

- The beliefs we have about ourselves today have been formed from the events of our past, some from very early in our lives. These beliefs can limit us or can drive us forward.

- Everyone makes poor choices some of the time. We will often learn more from our failures than from our successes as long as we take the time to reflect on what choice we made and what we can discover from it.

- The choices we make today will influence the future we will have. By choosing with that future in mind, we can shape the life we will have.

WIN OR LOSE, YOU CHOOSE 🥊

HOW TO BE A WINNER

HAVE THE COURAGE TO TAKE A RISK

He who is not courageous enough to take risks will accomplish nothing in life.

Muhammad Ali

To influence our future, we need to make different choices in our life today. Doing the same thing today as we did yesterday, running on automatic pilot, feels safe and secure. But creating a future based on our past – living without conscious choice and staying safely within our comfort zone – will only give us more of the same. Henry Ford expressed it nicely when he said, *"If you always do what you've always done, you always get what you've always got."* This is the life many of us live – sleepwalking from day to day, living with a background level of discontent and dissatisfaction.

It is only by doing something different that we can create a life of passion, power and purpose.

To live in a way that sees us winning more often means taking calculated risks. Those may be small choices such as going to bed earlier to get more sleep, with the risk that our partner thinks we're odd; walking into a gym, with the risk we'll be judged for our less than healthy physique; saying "no" to working this weekend because you want to spend time with the kids, risking the boss's disapproval.

They might be bigger risks – ones where you choose a radically different path in your life, such as quitting your steady job to start your own business or embark on a challenge to climb Everest.

If we make these choices, we can't be 100% certain of the outcome, so we have to accept the possibility of failure and consider the degree of impact it will have on us, our families and our future.

Choose to get out of bed 30 minutes earlier: Chance of failure is fairly low and the worst impact if we don't do it, is that we try again tomorrow.

Choose to go rock climbing without proper training: Chance of failure is pretty high and our life is at risk if we cock it up.

And, of course, one of the key components that prevents us from taking risks, is fear.

Fear can prevent us from responding, reacting or taking action. In physiological terms this is known as the 'Fight, Flight or Freeze' response. When your life is at risk, it's a good thing to have but in our everyday life it leads to one of three outcomes:

Procrastination – we are in a mental fight as we put off implementing the choice we've already made. We know we should act but we make excuses or do something else instead.

Denial – we pretend that we didn't really want to make that choice after all, fleeing from the risk and convincing ourselves that the future we know we want isn't that important.

Paralysis – we're so overwhelmed by fear that we don't know what to do and are unable to move in any direction at all.

Stop and Think

Does fear ever stop you? Does it ever get in your way?

And, when faced with fear, what is your usual course of action: Do you confront it? Embrace it? Challenge it? Or does it stop you in your tracks?

When you start to confront, challenge and overcome your fear, you'll be able to produce results in the face of any circumstance.

My first experience of fear

I'm 13 years old, and I'm preparing to box in the National Schoolboy Championship final. And I'm petrified! This fight is to decide who is the best young boxer in the whole country.

I couldn't sleep the night before… I couldn't eat anything… I'd never been so nervous.

My Dad, who had been my coach since I was eight, was helping me put my gloves on when I turned to him and said, "Dad, dad, I feel sick!"

He looked at me and said, "Bejeezus, whatd'ya mean ya feel sick?"

"I want to throw up!"

"I can't believe it! Dis is da final![5]"

"Bejeezus – go and be sick then," and he clipped me round the ear and sent me off.

I ran off looking for somewhere to be sick and I found some floor-to-ceiling velvet drapes. I went behind them and I threw up. Then I wiped the sick from my mouth and went back to my dad. I put the gloves on and stepped up into the ring a petrified young man.

And I stepped out a champion.

---

[5] My Dad is Irish – can you tell?

My life changed forever in that moment because I realised that if I could find the courage to step up, put myself at risk and be willing to fail, I could succeed. It was a pivotal moment for me and from then on, I learned to live with and manage my fear.

It doesn't mean I never experienced that kind of fear again. I have very clear memories of my second world title fight, waiting for my ring entrance, knowing that training hadn't gone according to plan and I wasn't feeling 10 out of 10. I stood there thinking "Oh, fuck…" but I trained myself to overcome that fear and was able to step up into the ring and fight.

KO Fear

What would it be like to fear less?

What would you do differently?

It takes heart, spirit and real courage to confront and overcome our fears. But if you can find the courage to choose to step up – to take yourself on – you will go beyond your current limits. Then, anything becomes possible. You too can KO Fear[6]

Since we've been talking about boxing – a sport where one really is putting one's life on the line – let's explore that a little more. I would step up into the ring, prepared to die. That doesn't mean that I was expecting not to come back out of the ring, but I wasn't oblivious to the risk either. It gives one a heightened experience of life and death. That takes huge courage – in the face of a worst-case scenario and still going ahead.

It isn't what I would focus on – where your focus goes, your energy flows – but it was there in the background.

It is in the management of all of those emotions and feelings that true winners arise. They have the ability to be able to deal with life and death situations.

---

[6] For those not familiar with boxing 'KO' stands for Knock Out.

> **Stop and Think**
>
> Take a moment to consider where in your life it would be helpful to have more courage: At work? In how you express yourself? In your relationships?

There may be several things running through your mind right now. Some will be in the immediate ("I wish I had the courage to say no to that unreasonable request from a client"), but some will be big picture stuff. They'll be your dreams and ambitions.

"I have a dream…" Hold that thought, we'll be coming back to him in a minute!

There will be things ticking along in the back of your mind that you've always wanted to do – but something stopped you. I'd bet even money that there is correlation between the area where you felt you wanted more courage and that unfulfilled dream.

The things we really want – the dreams and passions and purpose – that sit behind the person we show up as every day   become available the moment we make the decision to KO Fear.

To me, that's really exciting: the world of possibility that opens up when we step into the unknown. As a coach, the guys I work with are often pretty discouraged when they start with me. Some are in the depths of despair. As we work together, I see them gather up their courage, go beyond themselves and start to transform. It's a beautiful experience.

If they can do that, then so can you. Being able to confront our fear is an incredibly powerful tool and it means that we can produce results, for ourselves and for others, in any circumstances.

Wisdom from my teachers in life

When I left boxing, I had to find a new life. But things were different – I didn't feel the same. I'd lost the sense of certainty I'd had as a boxer. I was fragile and broken, and something deep inside was missing. I'd lost my passion, power and purpose.

I went looking for it in bottles and pills and purchases but none of it worked (big surprise) until, eventually, I got sick of it. I got sick and tired of being sick and tired, so one day I took a long hard look at myself in the mirror.

It wasn't pretty.

I had hit rock bottom and I told myself the truth. "You need to change."

I found the courage to start…

Most of the experts who have influenced my transformation have been products of the 20th and 21st centuries. One of the schools of thought I follow, however, is older – much, much older.

As I was travelling on my own journey to rediscover my passion, power and purpose, I was introduced to Stoicism. This ancient philosophy can be traced back to Zeno of Citium (300BC) and provides us with the idea that happiness comes from living a life of virtue – not from possessions or achievements. To live a virtuous life, in Greek, is *Arete*.

Stoicism starts with self-examination and questioning everything we think, do, feel and say. Talk about having courage! I can't think of anything more likely to invoke fear than having to take a good hard look at ourselves.

Stoicism recognises four primary virtues: Wisdom, Temperance (we'd call that self-control, these days), Justice and – you've guessed it – Courage. Even 2,500 years ago, wise men understood the importance of KO Fear!

They knew that, if we can just see how to reach them, we have the resources within ourselves to thrive and find happiness. But we first have to recognise that the vast majority of our life is outside our own control. There is nothing to be gained from bitching, moaning and whining, or from giving up when things get tough. What matters is making progress and living a life in line with natural order.

The stoic principles show up repeatedly in the winning traits I'm sharing in this book. They recognised that personal growth comes from within and from collaboration with others; they celebrate the journey over the destination; they urge you to eliminate toxic thinking and move through life without blaming or complaining.

Stoicism is as valid today as it ever was as a way of living your life.

The greatest breakthroughs come from taking a risk

Having the courage to take a risk can lead to some wonderful things. Consider some of the greatest breakthroughs in history, the greatest inventions and the greatest works of art and you'll realise that those responsible had to overcome fear to achieve them.

Think of the statue of David, for example, carved by Michelangelo. When he was commissioned to create the work, he chose a piece of marble which had been standing abandoned for 25 years. Two previous attempts to work the stone (by Agostino di Duccio and Antonio Rossellino) had failed, with claims that the stone had too many 'taroli' (imperfections).

Michelangelo, who was still early on in his career, created one of the masterpieces of the renaissance by not letting the opinions of others deter him.

The ability to KO Fear is even more important when it comes to social change. Think about the Suffrage movement of the early 20th century. Emmeline Pankhurst started The Women's Social and Political Union – a campaign which led to the right for women to vote. It caused national outrage and those who took part faced imprisonment for the civil disobedience they used to raise awareness of the campaign. It took almost 30 years for women to get equal voting rights with men (with the Equal Franchise Act of 1928) and during that time, campaigners risked their lives through hunger strikes and public protests.

No single act of protest, however, took more courage than that of Rosa Parks in 1955. Already part of the civil rights campaign, Parks refused to vacate her seat in favour of white passengers on a bus in Alabama.

When that white driver stepped back toward us, when he waved his hand and ordered us up and out of our seats, I felt a determination cover my body like a quilt on a winter night.

Rosa Parks

Even though this was only months after Emmett Till, a 14-year-old African-American, had been lynched after being accused of offending a white woman, Parks refused to move and, as a result, was arrested.

This led first to a boycott of the buses in Montgomery Alabama and, ultimately to the formation of a campaign led by Martin Luther King to end racial segregation. But Parks, an icon of the movement, lost her job, as did her husband, and was a regular recipient of death threats. The changes to civil rights that she helped to bring about, however, have shaped our views of equality ever since.

I'm not saying that you need to take life-threatening risks and seek to change the world. Start by looking at your own worth and consider what you could change for yourself, your family and your friends if you were prepared to stand up for yourself and KO Fear.

Let's not KO all fear!

Fear is not a bad thing, in the right setting. Ignoring fear when in a situation of genuine and uncontrolled danger (being held up at gunpoint for example) is not something I would recommend for a moment.

There are a few rare cases where damage to the amygdala (the part of the brain which processes memory and emotions) has eliminated the sense of fear and, as a byproduct, leaves the sufferer unable to recognise fear and discomfort in others. Psychopaths and sociopaths, as another example, get the chemical reactions of fear but don't worry about consequences. The result of these kinds of disorders can range from lack of respect for the personal space of others, to putting yourself and others in harm's way.

Fear is a basic animal response designed to keep us safe. It is all about the balance between risk and safety. And, if you get that balance wrong, you can pay for it with your life. I used to go into the ring with a mindset of 'kill or be killed.' Professional boxers face each fight with a willingness to die. And, sometimes, they die as a result of their sport. The same can be said of motorsports, horse racing, downhill skiing and plenty of other physical activities. Even angling, which is seen as a peaceful pastime, sees plenty of deaths and serious injuries each year.

In all of these cases, however, the risks are calculated and carefully regulated. In boxing, *three* people step up into the ring. Two boxers, intent on the win, and the referee who is there to make sure the rules are followed. He will decide if a boxer is unfit to continue fighting and if someone is using illegal or unsafe moves. His role is to regulate the match to make sure it is as fair and safe as possible.

So, it isn't a case of not being afraid – it's a case of understanding the risks and choosing to accept the consequences.

Exercises

1. What do you want in your life? What are your dreams and ambitions? Write them down to make a mental commitment to them.

2. Looking at those dreams and ambitions, consider where in your life you need more courage? Do you need to take more risks at work? Are you hesitating over taking bold steps in your personal life? Are there actions you know you need to take in your relationships where fear is holding you back?

3. Spend some time imaging your life without fear. What would you do differently if you were fearing less? What would you take on?

Summary

The second trait of being a winner is finding the courage to take a risk. When we face our fears and take action, we make progress towards our true dreams.

- Some of the greatest breakthroughs in history have come from people being willing to take a risk and do something out of the ordinary.
- If we live our life doing the same things we've always done, we'll never achieve our dreams. To follow our dreams means taking risks, but fear holds us back.
- Being able to confront fear is a powerful tool that means, whatever choices we make, we can follow through on them.

KO Fear

NEVER GIVE UP

The difference between winning and losing is most often not quitting.

Walt Disney

Even if you overcome your fears and choose to follow your dreams, things won't always go your way. Sometimes, your journey will be much tougher than you expected; sometimes your first attempt ends in failure; sometimes external factors will come along and change the game (the COVID pandemic of 2020/21, for example, had vast and long-lasting impacts for the whole world). A true champion, though, is someone who never loses sight of their goal and keeps on going, regardless of their situation and circumstances.

It's easy to say but, I know, it's really hard to do. When you are faced with disappointment or despair, and are gazing at an empty bank account, sitting alone in an empty room, or trying to run a business with no customers, me telling you to 'keep going' is likely to earn me a smack in the face.

Never giving up doesn't mean never feeling anger, disappointment or frustration. It's what you do once those initial feelings have passed that matters. It's what you then tell yourself. It's the difference between "I might as well quit – this is too much like hard work" and "Okay, what's my next step?"

Stop and Think

If you had the courage to fight for what you want and unlock and unleash the fighter within you, how would that change your life? What would you do differently. How would it make you feel?

Las Vegas, Baby!

I had a great start to my professional career as a boxer, winning my first 17 fights, all of which led me to win the British and Commonwealth Championships at the Royal Albert Hall. I was on the map. I was on the way to bigger and better titles.

At my first defence of the British title, the fight was stopped in round 7 because I had three cuts round my eyes. Ten months later I regained the title at the somewhat less salubrious location of Watford Town Hall.

The emotional rollercoaster ride that is the life of a professional boxer was well and truly underway. Over the next 12 months I defended my title five times, winning in exotic places such as Stevenage, Bethnal Green and Millwall[7].

Then I got the opportunity of a lifetime to fight for the World Championship.

Guess where?

Las Vegas!

Anyone who knows boxing will know that Las Vegas is the boxing capital of the world, so this was a big deal to a 25-year-old from Luton Town in his first professional fight abroad.

So there I am, walking down the Las Vegas Strip taking in the bright lights, the limousines, the big hotels... I look around, at the enormous venues. Elton John was headlining in one, Tom Jones in another. I think the Eagles were playing somewhere too and rumours were flying about that Frank Sinatra was planning a comeback[8]. I stood there thinking, "Wow, these are superstars." Then I reached the MGM Grand which, at the time, was the

---

[7] At the London Arena, to be fair, but it is in Millwall

[8] That's my memory of it, anyway. A true Las Vegas nerd might be able to tell me it wasn't Elton John, but Frankie Valli who was playing. The strongest impression I had was that these were big, big stars...

biggest hotel in the world and the host of all the biggest boxing matches.

I stood outside and I looked up into the air. There was a big display unit, 30 feet up in the air, complete with flashing lights. It read:

Billy Schwer, Luton

Luton?

Luton's on the map?

I don't know if you're familiar with my hometown of Luton, but it wasn't somewhere you'd ever describe as glamourous – and certainly not then! Luton in the early '90s was a bit rough round the edges. I stared at my name in lights thinking, "This is big!"

And it was. I was fighting defending World Champion, Rafael Ruelas from Mexico. He'd only ever lost one fight in his career and he was a familiar face in Las Vegas. The fight MC was Michael Buffer – famous around the world for announcing fights with, "Let's get ready to rumble…."

This was **really** big.

I was so certain I was going to win, I even put a bet on myself. I was so sure and I was determined to give it everything I'd got.

Until the fight started…

A few rounds in, *BANG!* Disaster – I got a big cut over my right eye. There was blood everywhere. Luckily, I had Denny Mancini, the best cuts-man in boxing in my corner. He patched me up and I continued to box on. I kept pushing and pushing and pushing – I wanted that title so badly. Two rounds later, *BANG!* Another disaster. I got a big two-inch cut – a gaping wound – over my left eye. The fight was turning into a bloodbath!

Denny worked his magic again and I carried on. I was trying to avoid Ruelas's punches but it was really hard to see them coming with all that blood in my eyes. The damage was bad. At the end of round seven I go back to my corner, sitting there, while my team work on me. The referee, Mills Lane, comes to my corner, and he looks at me. Then he looks at Denny working on the cuts. Then he looks at the damage and the blood flowing. Then he looks back at me again.

He says, "Kid, I'm gonna give you waan more raaand[9]."

I sit there and I think *"Shit!"* because I know that what he means is 'you've got to knock this guy out in the next round or I'll stop the fight.'

Have you ever felt under pressure to perform?

In that next round I gave it everything I had. It was a great round and a top performance from me. I won that round. But I didn't knock him out.

---

[9] That's my American accent, by the way!

So, the fight was stopped and my dream was shattered... as well as my nose (occupational hazard, I guess). After the fight, I remember sitting and waiting for the plastic surgeon to come and stitch up my face. That was one of the things I used to hate, after a fight – having to go get my face stitched up just after I'd had it bashed up. So there I was, broken nose, couldn't breathe, blood running down the side of my face, two big cuts over my eyes, body aching... I knew I'd been in a fight.

The surgeon started putting 70 stitches into my face and I thought to myself, *"Surely there must be easier ways to make a living. Maybe I should get a proper job."*

Never give up...

A proper job? I'd never had a proper job in my life.

I have a dream…not a job

Never give up…

Fight for What you Want!

If you have a dream, you've got to fight for it. You may not get it first time, or second or third… and sometimes those dreams can seem a long way off. An overnight success is incredibly rare. Just consider how long it took you to achieve some of your past goals – promotions, competitions, exams – and how much work you had to put in. It's not easy, is it?

One of the reasons that I'm an authority on how to be a winner is because I know how to lose as well as win. Of my 138 fights (both amateur and professional) I lost 31 of them. Not just in boxing either. I've failed in all areas of my life not only in the boxing ring: mentally… physically… financially… emotionally.

Of course, I could have quit after that defeat in Las Vegas. I could have settled, got a 'proper job' and lived a very different life. But it wouldn't have been **my** life.

Instead, I kept going and continued to fight for what I wanted.

If you want to know how to be a winner, learn from someone who knows how to deal with failure and loss.

What counts is the staying power to keep coming back after defeats. Even when 'shit happens' you need to keep going. And it does happen! Remember in chapter two I mentioned about my second world title attempt and things not having gone to plan? That wasn't my fault – it just happened. But I gave it my best and when I lost again, I kept going.

It's crucial to never settle. If you don't know what you want, or the dream you had is truly over, you just have to keep trying and searching and experimenting until you find your new dream. That was what happened to me, when my career was finally over in 2001. All those different careers I tried, were my search to find my new dream.

It took a while and some fairly random choices – and a divorce, bankruptcy, my home being repossessed and depressions – before I found that new life, but I kept fighting for what I wanted, never giving up until I got there. That's what you need to do too. When life gives you a KO and you are flat out on the canvas, get back up, move on and leave the past defeat behind you. All those different things I tried weren't my 'thing.' I couldn't find my thing and nothing felt right. But I persistently pursued my purpose. I stuck with it and here I am today doing what I love doing.

You got to fight for what you want. Get focused, get clear, and keep pushing forward.

Wisdom from my teachers in life

One of my early encounters with personal development was when I read Ekhardt Tolle's *A New Earth – Awakening to Your Life's Purpose*. I'd spent years trying to find a new life for myself beyond 'Billy the Boxer' and this book presented itself to me. It was the start of my journey back from a world of aimless searching.

For me, always a fighter, I'd been trying all kinds of different things up to this point – the endless random list of things that might work. Many others, however, as Tolle himself points out, are simply waiting for something to happen, instead of being prepared to take a risk. They are letting fear hold them back.

For them, the ego gets in the way, keeping us stuck in a life dictated by the outside world. We are driven by what Tolle calls the 'pain-body' which thrives on negativity and drama. It judges us in the context of how other people might react and draws on past trauma to shape our reactions. We're expected to get a 'proper job,' have a conventional family life and fill our lives and homes with whatever the adverts tell us to buy.

But in pursuing that material life, to the exclusion of all else, we lose sight of what we really want, and we define ourselves by what we **do,** not who we are.

That was the trap I'd fallen into. I was Billy the Boxer and when I couldn't box any more, I was lost. Whether you are a teacher or a nurse or an artist or a plumber, that's not just who you are as a person. That's not to say that your core purpose hasn't driven that career choice – if you believe you were born to bring comfort and care to others, then you'll naturally be inclined to work in caring professions – even if you didn't realise that was why you went down that route in the first place.

But our recognition of purpose gets lost very early on in life. Just cast your mind back to when you were little. How often did someone ask you, "What do you want to do when you grow up?" Already we were being expected to define ourselves by what we do. Early on, those career aspirations would have been unfettered by practical considerations – we want to be astronauts and roboticists and cuckoo clocks (every one of those is a real answer given by a small child, by the way). In fact, they probably give better clues to our true purpose (explorer, scientist, creator) than the 'sensible' careers we are later asked to decide upon.

Tolle's book is aimed at helping people regain that sense of our true purpose – starting by developing a connection to nature and the natural world to regain some inner balance. He advocates meditation as a means of stilling the mind and finding clarity, accepting what is and keeping our mind in the present instead of chasing material wants and getting caught in the constant chatter of our inner voice.

As we start to understand our deeper purpose we start to understand where there is imbalance in our lives.

You might have become a teacher because you wanted to shape young minds but, thinking you wanted advancement and more money, you chased promotion and now, as a school principal, find you are hardly doing any teaching at all. You might tell yourself 'it's just a job' and 'the money is good' but lurking in the back of your mind you know it wasn't how you expected life to be.'

[And that's not to say that many schools' principals aren't thoroughly fulfilled by their role – but their purpose might be to shape the way teaching is done or support others or even create efficiency. I merely use this as an example, again based on a true experience.]

So, Tolle shows, we must first be able to answer that fundamental question, "Who am I?" Then, by remaining in the present and seeing how ego pulls us in other directions, we begin to understand what is best for us regardless of what others may think.

This isn't an easy journey – you need to let go of a lot of the preconceived notions you've had about yourself – but it is worth the effort. Once you know who you really are, you know how you can best fulfil your purpose in life and that tells you what you need to be fighting for.

Three feet from gold – and other stories

History is bulging with examples of people who never gave up. From Richard Branson's multiple world record attempts to Helen

Keller's success as an author and activist despite being blind and deaf[10] or even Buster Merryfield who didn't become an actor until his 50s and finally found fame when he was 65, playing Uncle Albert in *Only Fools and Horses*. Even bestselling author Jack Canfield had over 130 rejections for his book *Chicken Soup for the Soul* before someone said 'yes.'

There are countless others. You can probably name a few of your own.

One great example of why you should always fight for what you want and never give up comes in the story of R.U. Darby and his uncle. During the Colorado Gold Rush of 1858 – 1861, Darby's uncle and later, R.U. Darby himself, staked a claim and had some initial success. After a while, however, they lost hope and sold their claim equipment to a local junk man. The junk man took expert advice and, three feet from where Darby and his uncle had been digging, came across a rich seam of gold and became one of the richest men of his time. This concept of being 'three feet from gold' as told by Napoleon Hill in his 1936 book *Think and Grow Rich* led Darby to never give up in his new profession and he became one of the most successful insurances salesmen of his time. The concept of *three feet from gold* has been used, ever since, as a reason not to give up and is even the title of a book on the subject.

---

[10] In an era which usually saw such people isolated and confined within the family

The opening quote for this chapter, comes from another expert in fighting for what you want – Walt Disney. At the age of eight, Disney first started drawing, copying cartoons from newspapers. He first launched his own animation studio in 1921 but within two years he had gone bust and Walt sold his camera to earn enough money to move to Hollywood.

With his brother he established the Disney Brothers studios and began to have some success with a character called Oswald the Rabbit. Then then there was a wrangle over the distribution rights and Disney and co-animator Ub Iwerks found themselves without most of their team or the rights to continue to produce Oswald.

That led him to Mickey Mouse – who failed to get any interest in the first two test pieces but, in adding sound (a first for cartoons) Disney finally had a hit.

You'd think it was all plain sailing after that, but no. Despite the growth in popularity of Mickey and Silly Symphonies, there was massive pressure on Disney and he had a nervous breakdown. Later, when he announced he was working on a full-length animated feature, the film industry dubbed *Snow White and the Seven Dwarfs* as 'Disney's Folly.' Production of the film was three times over budget and many believed it would bankrupt the company. We now know, of course, that it was a critical and financial success but of his next four films – *Pinocchio, Fantasia, Dumbo and Bambi* – only one made a profit and by 1945 company was $4m in debt.

It probably seems incredible to you now that someone who we associate with one of the most successful companies in history, had so many failures along the way but, as Disney himself said, the difference between success and failure is not giving up.

As for me, it took me four attempts, loads of stiches, fat lips, bruises and hospital trips, and another six years to get that World Championship title.

When persistence becomes stubbornness

As with anything in life, there comes a time when *Never Give Up* is no longer the right advice. If I hadn't given up boxing when I did, I probably wouldn't be alive now, to share my story with you.

I know plenty of people who continued on a path that was bad for them or not working, where they stuck it out, not from persistence but from sheer bloody-mindedness. The difference, I think, is that fighting for what you want is a different thing to being too afraid or too angry to change course. That's why this trait comes **after** the chapter on having courage and KO Fear.

A relentless refusal to take a different path or, worse still, the determination to change other people (that's never going to work) can lead to all kinds of disasters.

In my work for the Samaritans, I sometimes find myself listening to someone who is remaining in a toxic environment because they have tried to create success where there is none to be had.

Domestic violence is a classic example of this. The abused partner will remain in a relationship for years, hoping that things will change and believing that leaving would be giving up – and yet, if they were willing to take the risk and walk away, life for them and (often) those around them would be vastly improved.

So yes, fight for what you want, but be very sure that what you are fighting for **is** what you want.

Exercises

1. Do you know what you want? Write it down in detail and be specific about what that looks and feels likes.

2. Where might you hit difficulties in achieving that goal – where are the fights that you might have to have on the way to success?

3. Map out actions you can take – daily work and milestones along the way – to overcome the obstacles and to keep you going when you feel like giving up.

Summary

The third trait of being a winner is to never give up. Things won't always go your way but, if you have a dream, the only way to achieve it is to keep going.

- A true champion is someone who can bounce back from adversity, setbacks and defeats and keep going.
- To get what you want in life you have to be prepared to never settle or give up until you are living a 10 out of 10 life.
- Staying power is a vital ingredient in achieving any dream – being persistent and getting back to it after a setback.

FIGHT FOR WHAT YOU WANT 🥊

FOCUS ON THE FUTURE, NOT THE PAST

Stop being a prisoner of your past.
Become the architect of your future.

Robin Sharma

We all make mistakes. Whether it's something small, like tripping during the school play or something huge like ordering the Charge of the Light Brigade[11], we can't undo what has been done.

So many of us, though, base our decisions about our present and our future on past results. Even those small embarrassments in

---

[11] Considered to be one of the worst mistakes in military history –
https://en.wikipedia.org/wiki/Charge_of_the_Light_Brigade#Evaluation

childhood affect the choices we make, potentially for the rest of our lives. I decided at five that I was weak. It led me to need to prove myself as strong in the boxing ring.

The trouble is our past can end up **being** our future. If I was still clinging to that idea that I was weak today, the choices I make now would be quite different. I'd still have something to prove to the world and have a desire to win over other people, instead of winning in my own life.

Our future is not ordained by our past. We can choose not to let those past events to shape our decisions. We can KO Fear that doing something different is going to be riskier than doing the same as we've done before.

Stop and Think

How has your past shaped the decisions you are making today? Are there choices you are hesitating over because of something you decided about yourself or a previous experience you've had?

Henry Ford is credited with saying[12]: *If you always do what you've always done, you'll always get what you've always got.* I'm sure you can see the sense in that idea – that if we want a different result, we need to do something different.

---

[12] Like many quotes, it is almost certainly mis-attributed. The first definite citation was in 1981, 34 years after Henry Ford died…

You have the opportunity to design and create an exciting future. It doesn't matter where you're at in your life or what you are doing right now. If you are moving towards that designed, created future, you are going to feel inspired and excited by everything you do.

Stop and Think

What is the future you want to create? What is it like for you? How does it make you feel? How does it impact everyone else you encounter?

Focusing on the future rather than the past means you can be powerful in the face of adversity, setbacks and defeat, and let go of regret.

Just remember, you are only ever as good as the future you are living into.

Are you ready to live your life on your terms, by your design?

Going the distance

I come back from the defeat in Las Vegas, heal up and get back to work. Having challenged for the world championship, I've moved up the European rankings and I'm now ranked number one and next official mandatory challenger[13]. Off I go to Spain and I

---

[13] That's a big deal in boxing…

challenge and win the European title in Zaragoza after an epic contest[14] with the Spaniard, Oscar Caño.

I bring the title of European Champion home and defend it three times moving me back up the world rankings. Now I'm ranked number one in the world and I can challenge for the world title for a second time.

Wembley Arena, November 1999, and I'm fighting the very best: Stevie Johnston.

He was brilliant. He was like lightning. It seemed as if I couldn't catch him. The first half of the fight was brutal. Do you ever feel like you are having a bad day at 'the office'? That was one of them

---

[14] Voted "fight of the year" by the European Boxing Union

for me. And the second half of the fight was pretty similar to the first. He hit me so many times, I thought I was surrounded.

We go the distance – the full 12 rounds. There I am, waiting for the decision.

The judges are adding up the score cards… Those last few minutes. Phew!

"Ladies and gentlemen – the winner is….

"Stevie Johnston!"

Bloody nightmare!!!

That wasn't the end of it though because, after the fight, Stevie Johnston had a positive result in a drug test. But the positive test had been carried out in the same lab as the previous negative one – which breaks the WBC rules, so they refused to recognise the positive test[15].

Johnston got off on a technicality and I was so disappointed. He went back to America with his belt and I went back to Luton with more stiches in my face. I've had more stitches in my face than a patchwork quilt.

I had missed out, again. I was gutted…

---

[15] https://www.independent.co.uk/sport/general/uk-chiefs-stevie-johnston-stripped-of-world-title-283456.html

Have you ever felt cheated? Do you ever feel that life's unfair? I certainly did.

But that experience taught me something really important. To win more often and produce world class results, I needed to be powerful in the face of adversity, setbacks and defeat.

Roll with the Punches

If you only take one idea from this chapter, this is the thing to get: you have to take full responsibility for your future and choose where you focus your attention.

Have you ever just missed out on something? A promotion maybe, a pay rise, a relationship, the life you want...? Of course you have. We **all** have. You have to be ready for adversity, setbacks and defeat because they're coming your way.

Now is your chance to choose – who do you want to be when tough times come your way?

In life, to move on, we need to leave the past behind us and not dwell in it. If you spent too much time dwelling in the past the chances are, you'll get stuck there. You'll live a life constantly looking backwards and, if you're always looking backwards, you can't see where you're going and you're going to crash. That won't be pretty.

Now, I'd be willing to bet that there isn't a human alive who doesn't look back on past events and think (as my manager Mickey Duff used to say), *Could've, Would've, Should've...* It's perfectly natural but we've got to keep focused on where we're going. That's the lesson I learned from that defeat from Stevie Johnson and it's the lesson I want you to take away.

Keep looking forwards, take the lessons and learnings from the past and keep moving. Keep fighting for what you want – no matter what. That's not to say it will be easy or you won't need courage to let go of your past. Just don't end up being a victim to it.

When I was going through my tough time, I didn't have a future. I was living in a sort of abyss of darkness clinging to a past that no longer existed. That fed into the present moment and led me to desire to escape from how I was feeling. I just wanted to feel 'good.' That was why I tried all those different things that failed. I fell into depression. It took everything I had to let go of the past and change that perspective.

Life isn't perfect but if you can be responsible for the future that you're creating, designing and generating, the past will no longer have a grip on you. You'll be constantly moving towards somewhere that you want to get to so you will feel different about yourself. That's what I found. Along the way, you might get punched in the face a few times (hopefully metaphorically), but if you can roll with those punches, their impact lessens and you can move past them, regroup and come back stronger.

By now, as you've been reading this book, you may have realised that things need to change for you in your life. Maybe now's the time to have a look and see what work you need to do on yourself, because anything is possible.

If you connect with yourself, look inside and design and create an exciting future for yourself, it will influence your choices, give you the courage and energy you need to make changes in the here and now. Then you will be able to live life on your terms.

Wisdom from my teachers in life

As I went through my transformation, one of those whose teachings I studied was Werner Erhard. I enrolled in the Landmark Forum which was based on *est* (Erhard Seminars Training).

One of the most powerful aspects of this is the importance of 'having an experience' – rather than just completing some training. We are all unique and how we experience things can differ widely. That's why, for example, one person who has their dream career cut short is able to move past it and carve out a new life while another can spiral down into depression (as I did). How we *experience* that loss of identity and grieve over what isn't meant to be, is vastly different.

Erhard's training leads one to look at the experience of being yourself – how you act, what influences you – and to be aware of who you really are. It's deep and challenging.

There are some spiritual elements to his teachings. Erhard believes that we create our own universe – reality is what we create, not something that comes from the outside – and this means we are 100% responsible for everything in our own lives.

If forced to synthesize briefly the 'message' of the training … I'd say this: You are totally responsible for your life: you are the cause of all your experience. 'Responsibility' in est terms, is defined as 'the willingness to acknowledge that you are cause in the matter.'

Marcia Seligson, *Cosmopolitan Magazine*[16]

That is a powerful idea because it means you can choose how you respond to everything and influence the outcome of every aspect of your life.

But here's the catch (there's always a catch, isn't there?). If you are 100% responsible for everything that happens in your life it means you have to **accept** responsibility for everything that has happened in your life. It is all down to you. No more, "a bigger boy told me to do it" or "the technology failed me" or "the universe has it in for me." Sorry, but everything comes down to the choices you

---

[16] http://www.erhardseminarstraining.com/est-the-new-life-changing-philosophy-that-makes-you-the-boss/

have made and how you have reacted to people, events and opportunities. And, when the actions of someone else has an impact on you – an external event you didn't ask for and didn't expect – then you have to take responsibility for your reactions and responses to that event.

So, as you take responsibility for your past, you need to confront how you have acted, have compassion for the mistakes you've made and, in some cases, make amends. Only by doing this, can you let go of your past and make commitments for a better future.

The commitments you make have to be made from a place of authenticity. By knowing who you truly are, you are able to make choices and find the courage to take the calculated risks you need to take to move forward.

With this, you can hold yourself accountable for the commitments you've made to yourself and to other people.

How do you keep getting back up when life knocks you down?

Shit happens and it happens to us all. What's more, it has always happened. There is a Japanese proverb, *Nana Korobi Ya Oki* which translates (loosely) as 'Fall down seven times but get up eight times' and in the Old Testament of the Bible there is a very similar proverb. So getting up and keeping looking forward and moving ahead is a concept which has been around for thousands of years.

There are plenty of examples of those who might never have reached our attention had they not kept their focus on the future they wanted. Fred Astaire had an early screen test at RKO who described him as "Can't act, slightly bald, can dance a little.[17]" What a good thing he didn't decide to give up and go back to his career in Vaudeville.

JK Rowling saw herself as a failure in 1993, living on social security and "as poor as it is possible to be in modern Britain without being homeless." In the next three years she was divorced, suffered from depression and even contemplated suicide. But Harry Potter was already taking shape and kept her going until, in 1997, it was

---

[17] This has over time been extended into "Can't sing, can't act, slightly bald, can dance a little" but these additions first pop up in articles in the 1970s

published. Even then she was told that she'd never make any money writing children's books. Yeah – right!

Ludwig Van Beethoven who was being hailed as the successor to Mozart began to lose his hearing at the age of 28. He continued to compose for another 27 years until his death and some of his most well-known and powerful works were written after he had lost all hearing. Talk about rolling with the punches.

Since I'm a boxer, I rather have to make reference to Rocky – or rather, to Sylvester Stallone's commitment to his dream. Inspired by the Championship bout between Muhammad Ali and Chuk Wepner, Stallone wrote the script for a movie about an underdog given a shot at the world championship (because that happens all the time…). ABC bought it as a TV movie but wanted a rewrite. Not willing to let his story be reworked by someone else, Stallone (with help) bought back the rights. Several other studios were interested but Stallone kept insisting that he should play Rocky – so he kept getting turned down. Hanging on to that dream and never giving up was what launched Sylvester Stallone's career. And whatever you think of him and the film (don't get me started) it is a great example of someone fighting for what they wanted.

But, by far the most amazing example of someone who rolled with the punches of life must be Christopher Reeve. Reeve was a big star. He was Superman – literally – in four movies from 1978 to 1987. He was enjoying plenty of acting roles and starting to get opportunities to direct as well as enjoying his hobby of showjumping. Then in 1995 he fell from a horse, broke his neck and was paralysed from the neck down.

What would you do in a situation like that? What can anybody do?

What Christopher Reeve did was use his fame to raise awareness of spinal cord injuries and raise money to further research into treatments. He continued to campaign for the rest of his life and the foundation he put his name behind continues to seek cures for spinal cord injury.

You make your own luck

When faced with disappointment, of course you need to roll with the punches, let go of the past and move on. But if you are too future focussed, there is a risk that you won't learn from the past and that you won't be present in the here and now.

There are, of course, extreme examples of those who simply focus on one possible future and keep going regardless of the past. Compulsive gamblers, for example, can only see one possible outcome – the one where they win a fortune – and as a result, keep on gambling, disregarding the losses and telling themselves it will all be put right by that one big win.

There is also a balance between daydreaming – about what life would be like if you were picked out of the crowd to become a movie star – and being a dreamer, when your strategy for life depends on that random chance of being noticed. If becoming a movie star is your dream, you need to put in the hard work and create the opportunities, not just sit back and expect them to come to you.

Have you ever heard the saying "I'm a great believer in luck, and I find the harder I work the more I have of it"? There are plenty of variations on this idea but if all you do is sit back, focus on a future and hope that it will come, you are going to be disappointed.

There is another risk in ignoring your past and only moving forward. Failure to express and explore past disappointments and frustrations isn't all that healthy. In psychological terms the extreme of this is repression, where negative thoughts and feelings are completely blocked unconsciously. This does sometimes happen in the case of trauma – plenty of people say that they have no memory of a serious car accident, the mind having blanked out the most traumatic moments of the incident. In most cases it is an internal defence mechanism, the mind protecting itself from something it is not ready for, or able to process, but it can cause more problems later on if not addressed.

A more conscious version of this is suppression – the *don't think about it and it will go away* approach to a difficult event. The problem with trying to ignore a difficult thought is that it can make things worse.

Don't think of a white bear…[18]

Now, what's the most dominant thought in your mind? A white bear, right? Because the mind chases after the most obvious thoughts presented to it.

If I'd tried to ignore the disappointment of losing that world championship because of a technicality; if I'd ignored it altogether and pretended it never happened; if I'd supressed the frustration I felt at the time and buried my feelings instead of raging for a bit before moving on, I'd have run the risk of spiralling down into a deeper level of frustration.

Disappointment, frustration and anger are all natural responses to feeling cheated, losing out or having a dream shattered. It's okay to feel that way, just accept that you can't affect the past, know when to let them go and put your focus into the future you want to create. It's all a matter of balance.

---

[18] This is the "White Bear Problem" – a 1987 study by Daniel Wegner, published in Journal of Personality and Social Psychology (Vol. 53, No.1)

Exercises

1. What is the future you want to create? How much of your attention is on that future, rather than the past? Write or draw a description of your future and put it somewhere you'll see it every day.

2. When in your life have you felt disappointed or cheated? How did you react at the time? Which were your most common feelings? Write down those typical reactions and then describe how you'd like to react differently next time a similar disappointment comes up.

3. Are there situations or past events that you find it hard to let go of or move on from? What small steps could you take today to put your attention on the future? Make a commitment to take those actions and set aside the time you'll need to complete them.

Summary

Trait number four is to focus on the future not the past. If we spend our lives looking backwards and remain stuck in the past, we will struggle to move forward.

- Our past does not have to shape our future but that means we need to learn from past events and move on, rather than continuing to cling to them.

- You have to be powerful in the face of defeat and take responsibility for your future.

- You are responsible for everything that happens in your life – and you need to **take** responsibility for everything that happens in your life.

ROLL WITH THE PUNCHES

HOW TO BE A WINNER

BE RESILIENT IN ALL AREAS OF YOUR LIFE

I've missed more than 9000 shots in my career. I've lost almost 300 games. 26 times I've been trusted to take the game winning shot and missed. I've failed over and over and over again in my life. And that is why I succeed.

Michael Jordan

Resilience: one of those words that has been knocking around for centuries but has become really popular – almost overused – over the last twenty years or so. I've always seen it as a winning trait because, whatever walk of life you are in, you will be faced with setbacks. Resilience is the tool you need to overcome those setbacks, to accept what has happened and to cope with the situation that has been created. Resilience is what keeps you moving forward, toward the future you have defined for yourself (as covered in the last chapter). Metaphorically speaking, life is coming at you. Full blast, day after day, month after month, year after year... events, accidents, surprises... It just doesn't stop. You're going to face adversity, have setbacks and suffer defeats. Life is not perfect.

Knowing the future that you're living into is what will have you overcome them. That's what will give you the courage to keep moving forwards.

That's why I feel like I'm living a 10 out of 10 life. Because I'm responsible for creating and designing my future. Even though my life isn't perfect, I am happy, fulfilled and satisfied while I'm living it.

Some of the challenges we face are within our own control, when we make a bad choice or take a risk that doesn't come off. Others come from outside our direct sphere of influence, when someone else makes a decision that has a direct impact on us, or something happens in the wider world that changes the game for us and for others. But regardless of whether you took the leap and decided to quit your job, or an economic downturn sees you made redundant, the need for resilience is the same.

Stop and Think

When have you faced a challenge that interrupted your plans? How did you recover from the setback and get going again? What did you draw on to give you strength?

What is often misunderstood about resilience is that it isn't the same as endurance. It's not another way of fighting for what you want – which we covered in chapter 3. It's not the 'keep going' that matters, it's the ability to recover, learn from the experience and reset your focus. Resilience is the 'what's next?' question.

Third time lucky?

After that second failed attempt at the world title, I'd recognised the importance of being resilient and powerful in the face of adversity, setbacks and defeat. I realised that I had to leave the past in the past.

When I lost that second attempt at a world championship, I spent a bit of time caught up in 'blame and fault' thinking. I kept thinking, "I'm going to take him to court." But in the end, I realised I had to let that go. I had to carry on creating *my* future.

So my team and I regrouped and we got back to work again.

I had to wait a year for my next shot at a world title. My third attempt, at Wembley Conference Centre, was against a guy called

Colin Dunn. I was so certain I was going to win this time because I knew Colin and I knew I had the beating of him.

It's a full house; the crowd is roaring; the bell goes for the first round. In the first half of the fight, it's going beautifully. I start to build up a nice points lead. I have no cuts this time; there's no blood; everything's going great. I start thinking, "Yes, this is a third time lucky. Yes!"

Have you ever noticed that, in life, things don't always go the way you want them to?

Colin wasn't going to give up his title without a struggle. He fights his way back. He battles away and the second half of the fight becomes really, really close. I go back to my corner after 11 punishing rounds and sit down. I'm absolutely exhausted.

My boxing trainer Jack Lindsay – or gentleman Jack as I liked to call him – starts talking…

Jack was not your stereotypical boxing trainer. He liked opera. He used to paint and draw. He was softly spoken and he could hold a conversation on any subject. He was pure class, a true gentleman.

He whispers in my ear, "Billy, all you've got to do is survive. Three more minutes; one more round. Then you will have achieved your dream; you'll be crowned the world champion. You're doing fantastic. He hasn't laid a glove on you."

And I look at Jack, and say, "In that case Jack, watch that referee, because *somebody's* knocking the crap out of me."

I come out for the 12th round like it was the first. I give it everything…everything… The bell goes, the fight's over and we go to the centre of the ring, awaiting the decision. Here I am again – standing and waiting. The referee grabs hold of my wrist, and he tightens his grip. I think, "He's going to raise my hand in victory…"

"Ladies and gentlemen, the winner is … Colin Dunn."

Third time *unlucky.*

It was such a close fight. I lost on a split decision. It could have gone either way. After three failed attempts at winning the world title I really started to doubt whether it was possible.

Take it On the Chin

It's tough out there and sometimes you've got to take things on the chin. Defeat is our opportunity to rise up, step up and not quit.

If you really want something, you need persistence and courage. You have to keep experimenting, trying things out and failing. I'm good at failing. I believe in failing your way to the top.

Setbacks come in many forms. Some are external challenges such as a top customer cancelling a contract. Some are physical – getting injured or sick. Others are emotional when you find yourself caught up in anger, doubt or anxiety.

When faced with a failure or a setback, how do you reflect, recover and reset?

Some people face a setback by having a rant, slamming doors and swearing. They let go of their negative reactions with loads of explosive energy. If that's you, just make sure you know how to let go of the anger and violence – head to the gym and do a few rounds with the bag, pull on your trainers and run or just say 'enough' and let it go.

Other people want to lick their wounds in solitude, taking themselves off to a quiet corner of the office or go for a walk to reflect on their disappointment or frustration. As long as you don't let things fester and carry the burden around with you, this works too. You might do something different: pick up a phone and talk it through with a mate; distract yourself by going to the movies or losing yourself in a good book; laugh; scream; cry... These reactions – all perfectly normal – are part of the Mental Boxing match every one of us experiences every day.

Know for yourself how you let go of the past and reset your path towards the future you have set. Focus on the Future – Not the Past. That was chapter four, remember? Your view of yourself in the future is what creates the tension to drive you forward. And the more resilient you are, the easier it is to regain that tension when things don't go to plan.

As you work through a challenge, never forget that your thoughts affect your behaviour and the key to being resilient in the face of adversity, setbacks and defeat is to think about them differently. With an attitude of forward motion, you can then adjust your plan, look at the next best actions and get going on the way to your future once again.

Wisdom from my teachers in life

When it comes to resilience, my best teacher has been myself. Life as a professional boxer is full of setbacks and upsets and defeats. When I think of all the mistakes, the challenges and the cockups, I realise that I've had to learn resilience for myself.

When you are in a fight – whether it is to defend a title or as the challenger – and you get to round eight, nine or ten, you have to find a way to renew your energy as you enter the ring for the next round. You have to dip into your reserves and find the resilience you need to go again. That resilience has been learned from years of training and conditioning to get ready for each fight. You prepare yourself to have a mindset that allows you to keep going.

You can be sitting between rounds, and you've been beaten up and you know you are behind on points. Somewhere from within you, you must dig deep and summon up the strength to continue. Some of that strength comes from your training – physical conditioning in the case of a boxer – but it applies in any walk of life. By conditioning your mind, body and spirit you can find the resilience you need to keep going and be driven towards the exceptional. Finding the energy you need, you are drawing from past experience, training, personal development and, above all, your will. That gives you the drive you need, both the conscious and the unconscious.

For me, my main driver as a boxer was to prove that I wasn't weak and that I was good enough. I didn't know it at the time, but that was unconsciously getting me to come out, round after round, even when it was really, really tough. That drive also comes into play when things are going well. If I was ahead in a fight, I used that drive to build momentum – I'd be 'stocking up' on energy and resilience, using it to turn on the power and using it to overcome my opponent.

In boxing, anything can happen at any time. All it takes is one punch to change a fight. When you are fighting, you're on red alert all the time and when things are not going so well that's when the real test comes and the championship mindset really kicks in.

I've always thought of boxing as a battle of wills. In a boxing match, you are looking to break the will of your opponent, just as he is looking to break yours. It's a clash of wills and you are both looking to capitalise on any flaw that the other one may have. That's the brutality of boxing – you have to have that willingness to break your opponent.

In life outside the boxing ring, your opponent isn't another human being – it's the challenges that life presents. When life is going well, build momentum and recharge your mental, physical and spiritual stores. You know that the unexpected can happen at any time and you are readying yourself for the next setback.

> **Stop and Think**
>
> When we are faced with an obstacle, we can draw on those reserves you've built up to seek out a path through the difficulties.
>
> Where are the 'weak spots' in that challenge that allow you to find a way through its defences and on to victory?

Resilience is the ability to flip the switch and do what is required, moment to moment, and get the job done in the best way possible.

That's what makes you a winner.

Light bulbs, obstacles and world change

What's the difference between never giving up (chapter three) and being resilient? Think of them as two stages in the same process of facing failure.

Thomas Edison, for example, is reported to have had over 1000 failed attempts at creating a filament suitable for an affordable long-lasting light bulb. After each failed attempt, he chose not to give up. But he didn't keep on hammering away at the same idea, over and over, hoping for a different result. No, he used what he had learned from his previous attempts to fine tune the next attempt, or even to discard one avenue of experimentation and try something completely different.

Want an example of someone more contemporary? Then let's look at Joe De Sena[19]. De Sena started out as a stockbroker but took to running up and down the stairs in his NY apartment to keep fit. He became interested in Iron Man events and ultramarathons. Then, when he and his team were trapped in a blizzard during one endurance race, he saw the difference between difficult and desperate experiences and developed the idea of a race with obstacles to test your resilience.

He called his race a Spartan Race and designed it so it was suitable for anyone who wanted to test their endurance – even if they didn't have 48 hours to spare to complete the usual long-distance races. That first race (which had eight entrants) has led to a worldwide sporting event and there are a range of different races to suit a wide audience. To complete a Spartan Race, even the 3-mile sprint requires a really strong will to succeed and for the competitor to draw deeply into themselves to keep going when they think they've got nothing left in the tank.

De Sena believes that "Obstacles make me Stronger" (though I don't know whether he coined that expression or borrowed the mantra from elsewhere). This idea is a great way to find resilience when you need it and a mantra that anyone can use.

---

[19] Not to be confused with Dr Joe Dispenza who we've mentioned elsewhere in this book

Obstacles Make Me Stronger, Obstacles Make Me Stronger, Obstacles Make Me Stronger…

As a measure of De Sena's own commitment to resilience, his reaction to the Pandemic of 2020 really sums it up. Spartan Races are wholly dependent on people coming together in large numbers, so the worldwide lockdown brought the company to a halt. A friend of mine who knows De Sena asked him how he was managing and De Sena simply said, "Hey, this is why we train."

But if we want to look for one of the great examples of resilience of modern times, you can't go far wrong in looking at the life of Nelson Mandela. When you examine his life, you see resilience at every stage. He was the first member of his family to be educated and, even as a student, was prepared to protest (in fact, he was suspended for a boycott against the quality of the food at his university and didn't complete his degree). He decided to study law and despite having a young family to support did so by taking out loans to allow him to study full time. He became involved in the ANC – formed to give political equality to black South Africans and, most famously, to overthrow apartheid – and led the party during a campaign of civil disobedience and protests in the face of an ever-increasing level of restriction from the government of the day. The challenges he faced seem incredible to us now, with multiple arrests and prosecutions and, in 1964, he was convicted of sabotage and conspiracy to overthrow the government. He spent 27 years in prison – during which time he was harassed by warders, subjected to hard labour and solitary confinement and banned from having newspapers. So what did he do? He took a correspondence course to get a UK law degree and campaigned for better prison conditions.

When he was finally released in 1990, at the age of 72, he wasn't done. He went on to negotiate the dismantling of apartheid and stood in the first multiracial elections in South Africa in 1994. He was South Africa's first black president.

The challenges he faced throughout his life took real resilience and the adversity he faced in his attempt to bring about real change will be remembered for a long time to come.

Step forward – don't just roll over

Resilience means accepting life's challenges and moving forward. That doesn't mean you have to be a victim of every rotten thing that happens to you in your life.

You have rights and you are entitled to be treated fairly. So, if you get an extension added to your home and it was badly built, with leaks and cracking walls, you have every right to be disappointed, but you don't have to roll over and pay the dodgy builder. Fight for what you want, right? That was the third trait. Just know when you are fighting for what you want and when it is time to move on from the frustration of it.

If someone cuts you up at the lights, it's okay to feel irritated. If you are still seething about it when you reach your destination two hours later, that's probably a sign you need to do some work on being more resilient in the face of minor adversities.

It's all a matter of balance.

We have probably all heard of situations where civil court cases go on for years and years, with appeal after appeal, mainly because neither side is willing to accept that there might be a middle ground. No one can ever win in a situation like that, except possibly the legal professionals who bill by the hour. And resilience in these circumstances comes from seeing that, however sure you are that you are in the right, there may be a different perspective to consider and to be willing to compromise.

Often, in these situations where someone has mistaken resilience for sheer bloody-mindedness, one or other party is heard to say, "It is a matter of principle." But, to quote Dorothy L. Sayers "The first thing a principle does is to kill somebody." Admittedly, that quote does come from a detective story, but you get the idea. I talk about 'kill or be killed' in the boxing ring, but if the other fellow is on the canvas, I'm not going to ignore the ref and keep on fighting. I don't *actually* want to kill somebody.

TAKE IT ON THE CHIN

Exercises

1. When you face an adversity, what is your default pattern (see 'Take it on the Chin' for some of the examples). Make a list of what you need to do to find resilience and move forward again.

2. Think back to a loss or mistake from your past. Write out what you did to adapt and move forward from there? Note what you learned that has been of benefit.

3. To make challenges easier to handle, what daily or weekly rituals can you put in place to prepare yourself for adversity? Plan out when in your day you will do these.

Summary

The fifth trait is to be resilient in all areas of your life. Some of the challenges we face are within our control and others are not. Either way, you need to acknowledge them, learn and move on.

- Resilience isn't about endurance; it is about the recovery and forward movement after a challenge.
- We all experience setbacks and all react differently to them. Understanding your own patterns will help you develop resilience.
- Failure is how we learn. You are not a failure because you fail – success comes from keeping going even when you have experienced a failure.

TAKE IT ON THE CHIN

HOW TO BE A WINNER

BE WILLING TO LOOK AT THINGS DIFFERENTLY

It is not the strongest of the species that survives, nor the most intelligent. It is the one that is most adaptable to change.

Charles Darwin

When you are experiencing a case of 'Third time unlucky' you may need to face the fact that resilience isn't going to give you everything you need. There is only so much responding and reacting, you can do. 'Never Give Up' and 'Being resilient in everything you do' will give you what you need to cope under pressure, but things don't always work out and you can't control all the variables. We are constantly changing, and everything around us is changing too. Some of the factors that need to be in place may no longer be possible, or the circumstances aren't right anymore.

It's time for a new perspective. That doesn't mean giving up on the future you are seeking but it may mean a change in your approach. You may need to take a look at the future you have designed for yourself from a different angle and seek out different versions of that future.

Explorer Roald Amundsen dreamed of being the first man to reach the North Pole, but someone reached it first, so he had to adapt his dream and invent a new future; one where he was first to reach the South Pole (which he did in 1911). You may find that there are different versions of the future you want. Each will achieve your ultimate dream. Knowing all the versions of your future comes from understanding what it is you are really seeking for your life and then considering all the ways you can achieve that.

Stop and Think

What is your dream life? What does it look like and feel like? How does it give you a 10 out of 10 life? What are some of the possible routes that will get you to that life?

One important thing to note about the future you are living into: the actions and decisions you take today will influence which version of the future you eventually achieve. And it works from both ends. The future you see most clearly will influence the actions you take today.

Stop and Think

Just imagine... you have in your hand a lottery ticket for next week's draw. Suppose you know for certain that your ticket is going to win you £5000. How would you act today? What different choices might you make?

What if was £1 million?

Or £100 million?

Notice how different outcomes make you feel differently.

Another hard day at the office

As a boxer, I was always looking for new opportunities, new angles and new ways of winning.

I remember one Saturday morning, I was sitting in my mum and dad's kitchen, scratching my head. I was thinking, "if I'm going to become a world champion, maybe I need to make some changes."

"I've been the British, the Commonwealth and European champion. There's just one title that keeps eluding me. I've failed three times. Do I have what it takes, Am I good enough?" I'll admit, I was feeling a bit sorry for myself. I found myself wishing... Wishing I was better, wishing I was different...

"What do I need to do differently?"

And the change that I needed to make was staring right at me. I needed to move up into the next weight category.

Making the Lightweight limit of 9 stone 9[20] was killing me. Boxers, like jockeys, have to make a certain weight. Sometimes, to achieve the required weight at the official weigh-in, boxers would starve themselves or become dehydrated – putting themselves in real danger. It was especially problematic since being dehydrated, it is now emerging, can leave the brain more vulnerable to concussion – already more likely for boxers who are being repeatedly hit around the head.

Being at the right weight for a fight meant I was always on a diet. Most of us have tried to lose weight at some time in our lives and it's easy in principle – we eat less and exercise more. Simple! But have you ever worked really hard to lose weight and it's made no difference. For me it was a nightmare.

So, if I moved up to compete as a light welterweight it allowed me to be 5 pounds heavier. Now it doesn't sound a lot, but it was a big deal.

In 2001, by making that change I got another shot at the World title. I met my opponent Newton Villarielle, from Columbia for the very first time at the weigh-in. We shook hands; I didn't speak

---

[20] 135lb or 61.2Kg

any Spanish; he didn't speak any English. We had nothing to say to each other but we both knew we would have a great conversation with our fists.

My fourth attempt. This is it. It's my opportunity.

I step up into the ring. The bell rings — the sound I've heard a thousand times. The fight starts, the battle commences.

I have a great start. Round 2, I hit him with a perfect right hand. Boom! He goes over and hits the canvas. And I'm thinking, "This is it. There's no way he's going to get up. If he gets up from that, I'm going home."

He gets up.

I don't go home.

We battle on, round after round, and I know I'm in the fight of my life. Another bloody hard day 'at the office'. The bell goes at the end of the 11th round. I go back to my corner and sit down. My body is screaming, my mind is racing and all I can think is "How can I survive one more round?" I've got my dad in my corner, with Danny Mancini and Gentleman Jack Lindsey. They are slapping me around the face, throwing buckets of water over me and giving me words of wisdom. Even Gentlemen Jack is shouting at me. They would have got more sense out of talking to the corner post because I am so dazed and exhausted that I'm not all there.

Then the bell goes, I stand up, my team disappears out of the ring and the referee summons us to the centre of the ring. "This is the 12th and final round." I touch my opponent's gloves. We look each other in the eyes. Three more minutes to glory or suffer defeat and disappointment again. And Winston Churchill comes to mind because he once said, "History will be kind to me, for I intend to write it."

I start that final round intending to write my history. I give everything; I push through the pain; I hang on for dear life. At one point I take a punch to the back of my head which leaves me in a haze. I keep pushing, pushing, pushing…

The bell goes, the fight stops, the agony ceases and I go back to my corner, barely able to stand. Then we're called back to the centre ring, for that agonising wait for the judges' decision. In that moment my career flashes before me – from a boy of 11 having his first contest to the here-and-now, 20 years and 137 fights later. I'm having another attempt at the world title in this boxing ring – the place that I know as home. I am comfortable in this most uncomfortable of places.

I look out into the crowd. I can see my mum who has been ringside for all of my fights. We're looking at each other. I can hear my sisters, Mandy and Lisa. I can see the guys that have supported me from the very beginning. We're like family.

So, have I done it? Did we do enough? And the crowd falls silent.

"Ladies and gentlemen, the winner is… Billy Schwer."

I eventually get to hear the words I've been waiting for all my life. For the fourth time of asking I eventually achieved my dream to become the champion of the world.

Jab and Move

There is a saying, 'Insanity is doing the same thing over and over and expecting a different result.' If the results you are getting aren't the ones you want, then maybe it is time for a change. One thing to consider is that the results you get don't just depend on what you do, but how you look at things. It's all a matter of lenses.

If the way you see life is through a lens of your past – believing that you don't deserve success in the future, or that, since you never had success in the past you won't have success now – you won't take the right actions to create the success you want! Why bother, after all, since you always fail anyway?

A lens of the present – accepting life as it is – is a more serene way to live. You can wait and see what happens and something will come along. It sounds good but are you living in the present or are you settling? Humans are wired to strive and aim for goals. We have an amazing ability to create alternative futures for ourselves (prospection), so simply sitting back and hoping something wonderful will come along seems a waste.

The lens of the future allows us to take those goals and future opportunities and make them happen. We see something we want; we act now to create the opportunities for it to happen and we see the results starting to come our way.

That's not to say that you should only look at life through a single lens. What you've learned from your past, what is happening for you now and what you want in the future can work together to help you find the right action to take.

Stop and Think

Pick something in your life that isn't working as well as you want it to. How can applying different lenses to it help you adapt your approach? Notice how, as you change the way you look at the problem, the nature of the problem changes (thank you, Wayne Dyer).

One vital thing to remember is that you can't do it on your own. Whatever your dream, whichever way you look at things, you need a team around you. In every chapter of this book, even if you haven't noticed it, I've been mentioning my dream team. My Dad, my trainer Gentleman Jack, my manager Mickey Duff, my cutsman Denny Mancini. They were an essential part of my world championship attempts. There were others too: fitness coaches, physiotherapists, osteopaths, masseurs, chiropractors, nutritionists, personal trainers… you name it.

When I was puzzling out what to do after that third defeat, they were all part of the decision to move up a weight class. Together we built a plan for how to move me up a weight (which isn't just a case of me sitting down and enjoying endless boxes of chocolates!). That world championship win was a team effort and an ongoing collaboration between us to get the result we all wanted.

Stop and Think

Who is in your dream team? For the future you want to create, who are the closest contacts you can confide in? Who is willing to fight alongside you? Who has got your back? And who makes up the wider team whose knowledge, expertise and support you will need?

The people you need in that team won't always be your friends. In fact, sometimes the adaptations you need to make will include adapting the team itself. By the time of that final attempt, I had moved away from Mickey Duff's management and was managing myself because that was better for me and what I wanted. It's not always easy to sideline those who have helped you in the past but things change and so do people. If the fit is no longer right or you discover you have people around you who are telling you want you *want* to hear, rather than what you *need* to hear, you might have to make changes.

The changes you need to make aren't always obvious to you. You can't see them, but other people may. So, learning to listen is at least as important as learning to make choices and set the direction.

If you can't immediately think of the people you need around you from your direct contacts, then it's time to consider getting yourself a coach. Is this me, slipping in a shameless plug for my coaching programmes and executive workshops[21]? Well, maybe a little, but since I retired from boxing, I've spent over two decades learning, experiencing and sharing what I do with others. I want to be a part of your dream team and I'd love you to be a part of mine. Really good teams learn from one another and help each other out. It is a two-way relationship.

If you are looking toward your future and wondering how you get there, it can take courage to make the changes you need to make. If you aren't sure how to get the result you want, you are going to need to take some risks and be resilient when you fail. And it's hard – but having the right people in your corner makes it all a bit easier.

Wisdom from my teachers in life

When I think about the people who have supported me and educated me in my life, my overwhelming feeling is one of gratitude. Every one of the teachers I've mentioned so far, those still to cover and those who haven't had a namecheck in this book but influenced me in other ways, are deserving of my love, acknowledgement and thanks.

The teachers I want to mention in this chapter, however, were the ones that helped me to see things differently in my life as a boxer

---

[21] You'll find more details on this at the back of the book

– from the very start of my career, right through to when I retired and, in one case, up to the present day. As a boxer, you are surrounded by a team, there to help you make it to the top – and it starts with family.

As I've mentioned, my dad was my boxing coach from when I started boxing at the age of eight and throughout my career. He'd been a successful amateur boxer himself[22] and was a business owner, earning his living as a welder. It was hard work, but Dad was always a grafter. As a kid I never really understood his drivers but he put everything into creating a great life for his family. Holidays in Spain, water skiing after school and, of course, the endless travel all over the country so I could compete. He showed me that, with commitment and hard work and a strong enough motivation, the kind of life I wanted (whatever that might be) was available to me. Because he ran his own business, I never knew of any other way to live, and I've always been entrepreneurial as a result.

He and my Mum were a team and that was where I first learned about the power of teamwork: Dad out working to provide for us; Mum at home as the glue for the whole family, managing everything. As a family, my sisters and I learned how to be a team and have been that way ever since.

---

[22] https://boxrec.com/en/box-am/1000525

When I was 11, with my first contest coming up, I remember being taken to London to buy my first pair of proper boxing boots. We went to the Lonsdale shop on Beak Street (just off Regent's Street) in London. It was a big deal because Lonsdale is a name that has been associated with boxing since 1891. We got to the shop late in the day, in a rush, and there, to sell me my first ever pair of boots, was Denny Mancini. It was the first time I met him, never guessing that when I became a professional boxer he'd be in my corner, as my cuts man.

From Denny I learned about loyalty. He was a gentleman, good fun to be around and a staunch defender of the rest of the team – and of me in particular. He would tape my hands up before a fight (boxers tape their hands up with zinc oxide tape as it protects them and prevents injuries to this most essential tool of the boxing trade). As he did, he would always bring a bit of levity to the changing room, knowing that the rest of the team might be nervous. Sometimes, the energy and personality you bring to a team is just as important as the technical skills.

Boxing is a vigorous sport and, by its nature, full of raw emotion and energy. It's easy to let everything run wild and lose focus, especially if, in that minute between rounds, I had cuts being dealt with and might be in a bout that wasn't going my way. It was from Gentleman Jack Lindsay that I learned how to find calm and control in the heat of the moment.

He'd been a trainer for 40 years – but it was a hobby to him. He trained kids at the Chapel Street Nursery gym in Luton. By profession he was a plumber and, as I've mentioned before, loved opera, art and history. The perspective he gave me, that you can be unconventional in how you live your life, has stayed with me my whole life. He was with me from when I was 17, training me right up until the end of my boxing career. I was a very different man when I first started working with him to when we finished in 2001, and it was an experience for us to grow together.

When I was 19, I was making good progress as an amateur boxer and, in one contest, when I was representing England against Germany I was approached by Mickey Duff. I won my fight in the second round and he gave me his card, and said, "Give me a call if you ever want to turn pro."

At the time, that wasn't on my mind because, as an amateur, there were opportunities to be a part of the Olympics and the Commonwealth games. It was another two years before I made the decision to arrange a meeting with him at his offices in Wardour Street, London. Mickey Duff was a partner in a company called National Promotions along with Terry Lawless and Jarvis Astaire. He always looked out for me but he really taught me about the business of professional boxing.

Whatever your profession, it pays to remember that it is a business – either yours or someone else's. Within the boxing world, the boxer is the commodity and part of your purpose is to sell tickets for your fights. A lot of the time, he'd be liaising with Mum and Dad who would be selling tickets from our kitchen table (with me hiding upstairs so I didn't get distracted by the people who were coming and going all day).

The conversations I had with Mickey were just amazing. He told me stories about all the fights that he had put together and about the business side of things. I became very interested in the commercial aspects of boxing. I would want to know what happened with the TV rights, so he'd explain how the TV companies would pay him as the fight promotor, that he'd get a percentage of the ticket sales and pass a percentage on to me.

It helped me understand my role in the business of boxing and, ultimately that, when your career is over, the business just moves on to someone else. I know lots of boxers – and other sports professionals – who have found that concept really hard to get their head around but it's the same in any business. It's not personal.

One other thing I learned from Mickey was good business practice. He was hard-nosed and he had quite a temper when provoked, but he was absolutely fair to me. I was always paid on time and paid the right amount (not always the case in boxing) and I came to see how good business practices pay off. Since recognising this, I've tried to apply the same fair-minded integrity to those I work with.

Teamwork at the South Pole, in space and closer to home

When it comes to great examples of human adaptability, the most amazing things happen at times of extreme challenge.

Explorer Ernest Shackleton assembled a crew for an expedition to the Antarctic using some very unorthodox methods, believing that camaraderie and teamwork mattered as much as technical ability. He was proved right when the ship Endurance became trapped in pack-ice. By adapting to the extreme conditions and a series of disasters, Shackleton brought his entire team safely home. During that time, they saw the loss of the ship, had to camp out on ice floes and live as castaways on an uninhabited Island. It took over 18 months for the 28-man crew to make it back to civilisation and is seen as one of the great stories of the era.

Another example of adaptability under pressure has to be Apollo 13. The NASA mission to the moon hit problems when an oxygen tank blew up, causing the loss of heating, light and water and also rupturing the supply line for the second oxygen tank. Ground crew and the team trapped in space had to rewrite procedures, invent equipment based on what supplies they had available and eke out their limited water to survive. It was an extraordinary feat.

The stakes don't need to be nearly so high, however. Yellow Pages had to adapt to the move to a digital world by becoming Yell.com and Netflix, a postal video rental company is now one of the leading digital video streaming businesses.

But I did also want to look closer to home when it comes to looking at things differently. I've already spoken about the team who worked with me to get me to the world championship. But what about since then? When the pandemic hit, I was working successfully as a coach and speaker, travelling around the UK to work with business leaders and organisations. Like most people in my field, that came to a dead halt with lockdown. We all had to pivot online and find a different way.

I needed help and was introduced to a small business called Creative Words (feel free to check them out[23]). They specialise in helping people like me and the owner Cate Caruth, and her team have been with me ever since, supporting me to update my coaching content, rewrite my website, build new marketing materials and get consistent with LinkedIn. And when I wanted to write a book?

What you have been reading is a perfect example of adaptation and teamwork. From my keynote presentation, Cate created the pages of this book and together we have honed it, polished it and published it. Never underestimate the importance of the right team when you need to look at things differently.

---

[23] www.creativewords.cc – if you decide to get in touch, tell Cate that 'Billy sent you'

It's all about balancing the traits

One of the most essential aspects of these seven traits that I've been sharing with you, is to see them working together. Usually, one is the most appropriate to apply in a given situation but they balance one another out.

So, sometimes, you need to look at things differently and adapt but, at the same time, you need to keep in mind that you need to keep going, even when things are tough. If you keep changing course every time you hit an obstacle, you'll end up flip-flopping from one thing to the next, never satisfied and always convinced that "this is it – this time is 'the one'." So yes, look at things differently, jab and move as needed but always remember to keep your focus on the future you want to create and never give up on that. You might need to find a different path, get help from other places, or see it in a different way but the destination remains the same.

Of course, sometimes you don't know what that future is – which is where I was when my boxing career ended. I was trying to find a new identity for myself so I tried lots of different things. That's also part of the balancing act – to give things enough of a try to be sure but to have the courage to say, "this ain't it," and try another path. Every new venture will give you an idea of the future you really want for yourself.

JAB AND MOVE 🥊

Exercises

1. Think about the dream future you have for yourself. Now make a list of the different ways that you can reach that future. Some might be wild and whacky, some more conservative but let your creativity play for now.

2. Using the list you made above, choose one option that has a good chance of success. Apply all the other traits to it and note down what choices you need to make, and where you need courage, persistence and resilience.

3. Who do you need in your corner as your dream team to make the option above a success? Write down who they are and how they can help you. Add to that when you are going to get in touch with them to invite them onto your team.

Summary

You need to be willing to look at things differently if you want to be a winner. That's the sixth trait. If things are not going in the right direction, you might need a different perspective or to adjust how you are doing things.

- Whatever dream you have, there are multiple different routes to get there, so be ready to adapt.

- An essential ingredient for adapting is the team you have around you. They will see your goal through different lenses as they apply their expertise to the problem.

- Always draw on your own experience of the path, your understanding of the present and your ambition for the future to guide your decisions.

JAB AND MOVE

HOW TO BE A WINNER

BE RESPONSIBLE FOR WHO YOU ARE – OWN YOUR LIFE

You must take personal responsibility. You cannot change the circumstances, the seasons, or the wind, but you can change yourself. That is something you have charge of.

Jim Rohn

So here we are at chapter seven – time for the big finish. That's something that I learned from boxing. When you are coming out for the final round, you always want to dig deep and find one last bit of energy to put on a good show - a flashy finish to impress the judges (that's you, in the case of this book!).

Let me ask you then: would winning – experiencing success – be something you'd like more of? If you are like most people, you'll be nodding right now. We want to win more often, we want more success.

To do that, however, means taking responsibility for yourself. Who you are today is a result of the choices you've made and the actions you've taken. Whether you have taken a risk, decided to keep going or changed course, the person you are today is down to you.

That's not to say that everything that happens to you is your fault. We are interacting on a daily basis with other people who are also making decisions and acting in ways that can have an impact on your life. But you are completely responsible for how you choose to respond.

Stop and Think

Here's an everyday situation. You are walking down the road and someone crashes into you because they are glued to their smartphone. What's more, they hardly bother to apologise and just keep going.

How do you react? What is your default response when that happens?

How would you like to react? What sort of person do you want to be in a situation like that?

We all have 'knee-jerk' reactions on a daily basis, as we are triggered by what is going on around us. Some of these impulses feel like they are out of our own control (remember those 'hot buttons' we mentioned in Chapter one?) – a situation happens and we just react. We may then regret it because it isn't the person we truly want to be. We don't want to snap at the kids or bicker with our partner but somehow it just happens.

In fact, these impulses which feel outside our control are habits and they *can* be changed. The first step is to accept that you are responsible for those reactions and you are responsible for changing them.

While you are still blaming the idiot who can't take his eyes off his phone for long enough to walk in a straight line, you are a victim of the situation and that is a pattern of behaviour that can easily send you into a spiral of 'poor me' victim-thinking. You even start seeing 'poor me' in perfectly ordinary events – such as taking it personally when it rains on a day you wanted to go to the beach, as if the weather 'did it on purpose.'

If you own your life, if you take full responsibility for your reactions and work to be more like your true self – the self you really want to be – for more of the time, you'll be able to come back again and again after defeat.

No one else can decide who your true self is. That's in your hands and yours alone.

Twenty years – and three months!

It took me twenty years to win that poxy belt! Twenty long years.

And shall I let you into a secret? Those images you see of me with the belt across my shoulder and round my waist, I can hardly remember. I was in such a daze that it was all a blur. In fact, I missed my own victory party because, on my way to the after-fight party I started to feel ill, experiencing double-vision and throwing up. I was shipped off to hospital and kept in while they checked me for concussion and brain damage.

It didn't matter – I'd made it. I was World Champion. I'd shown that I wasn't weak and I was good enough.

Three months later, I was back in the ring to defend my title. In truth, it was too soon. I wasn't okay and I ended up on my knees with the fight being stopped.

I was taken out of the ring on a stretcher, put into an ambulance and rushed to the nearest hospital. Boxing is a beautiful, brutal business. I lay there feeling scared. I'd stepped up into the ring that night, prepared to die and now, maybe I was about to.

That night, lying in hospital, I made the toughest decision I'd ever made. I was done. It was time to retire from professional boxing.

For twenty years, I'd been 'Billy the Boxer.' Now who was I? I've already written about the various different careers I tried after my boxing career ended – the constant searching for a new identity. And yes, I did also go looking for it in 'sex and drugs and rock and roll'. I was lost and I had no sense of a future or who I wanted to be. I was the victim of my own circumstances and was trying to fill the void inside me with 'stuff.'

That was how Mental Boxing came about – as a way to explain what was going on inside my head. It was only when I unravelled who I really was, working with teachers who could help me explore the experience of being me, that I learned to own my identity. I got a coach, then I became a coach and, as a result of deep work (work which is still ongoing now), I learned to live a ten out of ten life and to be happy, fulfilled and satisfied.

BoxClever

The smartest thing anyone can do, is to be true to themself. It can also be the hardest thing you have to do. We live in a world where we feel we ought to conform and chase the dreams that external influences tell us to chase.

As a young boxer, who was doing well in his career, I enjoyed money, fame, success... but they weren't what was really driving me. My driving cause was to prove myself – to show the world that I wasn't weak, that I wasn't a victim and that I was good enough. That kept me going throughout my career – until my career ended.

> **Stop and Think**
>
> What are your true drivers in life? What are the aspects of your life that are of greatest importance? Have you even stopped chasing the external goals for long enough to consider that?

If you are facing the same dilemma I was, when I'd achieved everything I wanted in my professional career and found myself out in the 'real world' asking myself "now what?" then I can sympathise. It's tough.

There are no easy answers to this. You need to address what has happened in the past, address any traumas that you have experienced and focus on healing yourself at every level. You will need to confront what isn't working in your life – however hard that might be – and accept that the life you want to live might not be the one you are living right now. There will be several aspects to this. Here are some of the things you should be asking yourself:

- Is your body in the best possible shape it can be to achieve what you want in life? Whatever else is important to you, if you don't look after your health, you won't be free to do whatever it is that matters most to you. To live a ten out of ten life, first and foremost you need to keep living!
- What are your daily habits and are they taking you in the right direction? Habits are a tricky thing because they are, by definition, things you do without thought[24]. You might know that pouring a glass of wine the moment you get home is reducing your desire to be productive in the evening but if it is happening without you even noticing it, it can be difficult to address. The first step is to recognise the habits you want to change. This activates the reticular activation system (a part of the brain that helps you home in on what is important) and you'll spot that habit before it kicks in.
- Are your relationships giving you what you need? This is a tough one because we don't always want to acknowledge that our friends, relations and life partners aren't giving us what we need. Even harder is admitting that you aren't giving them what they need. Some honest conversations might be on the horizon but if you come from a place of authenticity and an intention to make things better, you will end up in a better place for everyone.
- Is the work and career you are following in line with your values? Many of us work for a living (i.e. it pays the bills) but it is important that you are still a living a good life

---

[24] Some habits can turn into addictions which are even harder to address.

while you work. Of course, if your personal values are aligned with the work you do (civil servants, for example, often have strong service values) you'll feel fulfilled in the work itself. If that's not you, then be sure you can see how your job as a means to an end – which might be to give your kids the best or to give you the freedom to pursue a hobby or interest, or even as a stepping stone to a future career or opportunity.

- In every aspect of your life are you fully committed and doing your best? It is only too easy to put yourself on 'autopilot' and cruise through life. We've talked about settling in life before. If you want a life full of passion, power and purpose however, it will take hard work and the strength to push through when you don't feel like it. The same is true if you have to confront what isn't working.

Examining questions like these isn't a once-and-done exercise. There are many levels to taking responsibility for ourselves and you should be re-examining your life on a regular basis. In doing so, you will start to live in the present (instead of being trapped by the past) and choose how you want to live.

Knowing that things need to change and being ready to take the next step doesn't always have to be done alone. Never be afraid to ask for help, whether that is joining a support group to address an addiction, visiting a relationship councillor to give your marriage some help or engaging a coach to help you explore any and all aspects of your life.

Wisdom from my teachers in life

As I was in the process of owning my life after 'Billy the Boxer' I committed to the Compassionate Inquiry course of Gabor Maté. When it comes to taking responsibility, his teachings are key.

Maté's view is that body, mind and emotions are all interconnected at a fundamental level, which has two significant impacts on who you are today and who you choose to be.

Firstly, he sees that the environment we are in and the information we take in will massively impact our inner world. For example, suppose you decide to watch a horror film on TV. Even though that film is a fiction and no bigger than the size of your TV screen, it will trigger emotional responses in most people. With fiction, most of us are able to shake that off. It's not always so easy with fact. There are studies which showed that the media coverage of the Boston Marathon bombing of 2013 caused higher acute stress to people who watched the media coverage than those who were present at the time of the attack[25]. Our emotional wellbeing is under attack from excessive media consumption and each time we see something that troubles us, it triggers the 'fight, flight or freeze response' which has a direct impact on everything else.

Secondly, Maté explores how emotional wounds lead to physical problems. In other words, illness and pain. Modern medicine has

---

[25] https://www.pnas.org/doi/10.1073/pnas.1316265110

ght us to see physical ill-health in isolation. Our back hurts so we visit a physio or go to the GP for painkillers. Maté believes that the physical symptoms we experience can be triggered (or at least made more likely) by what is happening in our mind and spirit.

> **Stop and Think**
>
> Recall a recent time when you have been feeling a lot of stress, anger or anxiety. Can you remember how your body felt? Were you feeling tight across the shoulders? Pain down your neck? Clenching your jaw until your face ached? That's just the impact on the muscular-skeletal system. Just image what it is doing to the rest of your body functions as you flood it with warning hormones, restrict the oxygen flow or load it with processed foods and other toxins.

Some of the factors affecting us can come from childhood traumas. These might be Trauma (with a capital T – defined as events with significant mental impact such as a serious accident, physical or mental abuse, rape, profound loss or wars) but they are not the only influences here. 'Small-t traumas' (getting separated from Mum in a shopping centre as a nipper, struggling with maths in school or being teased by our siblings) can have just as much impact. And it affects us all and at every stage of life. COVID, economic pressures, debt, workplace bullying, difficult relationships… they all add up to trauma in Maté's view. So we develop coping mechanisms. We laugh it off, drive ourselves too hard, eat, drink, smoke… Anything to escape the negative conversations we are having with ourselves.

Healing, according to Maté starts by accepting the truth. For me, that meant accepting that I felt 'weak' because my sisters teased me at 5 years old. For you, there could be similar unexplored childhood memories that are still with you. The idea is not to blame or fall into self-pity but to recognise where your beliefs of today are coming from and how they affect who you are and how you behave. Then keep reminding yourself that your thoughts are not reality. Whether you think you are weak or stupid or not worth it, these are just the mental boxing that is coming from your past.

Okay, we lost!

In May 1997, the results of the UK general election showed that the Conservative Party had suffered a landslide defeat. It was a bruising experience after 18 years in power. Party leader and former Prime Minister, John Major, made a speech to the party faithful the following morning which was a great example of someone taking ownership. There is a link to the whole speech[26] in the footnotes but the most powerful aspect of it is the closing.

---

[26] https://johnmajorarchive.org.uk/1997/05/02/mr-majors-statement-at-cco-on-the-morning-of-2-may-1997/

So right, OK, we lost. So go away for the weekend, relax, fire yourself up again, and then come back. For when you come back at the beginning of next week, we have a job to do and we'll start doing it.

No nonsense, no blaming others, just acknowledgement of what had happened, what had been achieved and what came next. Whatever your politics, I see it as a great example of taking responsibility and owning a situation.

There are some other great examples of leaders who took responsibility for themselves and others. From Teddy Roosevelt's great statement, "If you could kick the person in the pants most responsible for most of your trouble, you wouldn't sit for a month" to Harry S. Truman's, "The buck stops here," there are plenty of case studies to draw on.

One story I particularly like of leading by example, however, is that of Russi Mody, who was MD and chair of the Tata Steel Company. Like many of these tales, it has probably been a bit distorted over time with retelling (and I'm about to add to that by retelling it again) but the message is clear.

Mody used to hold regular meetings with all staff at the plant in Jamshedpur and on asking if anyone had any concerns, one worker took up a seemingly trivial issue – the state of the worker's toilets. According to him, they were unhygienic and run-down. The executive toilets however, he complained, were always spotless. I'm sure you can recognise similar 'them and us' niggles in your own company.

Mody didn't dismiss it. He asked his executives what they needed to fix this issue and, on being told it would take month, wasn't satisfied. He summoned a carpenter and asked him to swap over the signs for the two toilet blocks – making the worker's toilets the executive block and vice-versa. He issued a standing order that the signs be swapped over every two weeks. It took three days for both toilets to be equally clean and functioning.

Mody owned the problem, was willing to put himself in the worker's shoes by having to use the sub-standard toilets and made sure no one ever forgot that they were all entitled to the same levels of care.

Responsibility isn't blame

The whole purpose of this trait is for you to take responsibility for everything that has happened to shape who you are. That does not mean it is your *fault*! If someone bullied you at school, you are not to blame for the actions of the bully – they are. What I'm saying you need to own is the choices you made as a result of being bullied. It was your reactions, the decisions you made about yourself at the time and how you allowed that experience to affect the choices you've made ever since, that define the person you are today.

The most inspiring of examples of this is probably Viktor Frankl. An Austrian psychologist from a Jewish family, he was sent to a concentration camp in 1942 where he spent three years and saw his family die as a result of the Nazi regime. His book, *Man's Search for Meaning* is a powerful description of that time and how ownership of his own thoughts and feelings gave him freedom. That's what we're talking about here.

The one thing you can't take away from me is the way I choose to respond to what you do to me. The last of one's freedoms is to choose one's attitude in any given circumstance.

Viktor E. Frankl

And it brings us all the way round to the first trait again. Taking responsibility and owning your own life gives you choice – Win or Lose, You Choose.

Exercises

1. What is your driving cause? Can you say or write your purpose – ideally in ten words or less?
2. What are the stories you tell yourself most often? Write a list of them and how they move you toward or away from achieving your future.
3. Who is the real you? Write a description of the person you truly aspire to be.

Summary

When you've mastered the other traits, you need to be responsible for who you are and take ownership of your life. In doing so, you gain complete freedom and control over yourself.

- Who you are today is a result of the choices you've made and the actions you've taken. This creates the unique experience of being you.
- We live in a world where we feel we ought to conform, but what is right for others may not be right for you and fitting in could be the worst thing you can do for your long-term happiness.
- Everything is connected: body, mind, emotions… you need to look after them all. Ignore any one and the other aspects of who you are will suffer.

BoxClever 🥊

HOW TO BE A WINNER

NOW WHAT ?

Over the course of the last seven chapters, I've shared with you the seven traits to being a winner in whatever your walk of life may be.

But what do you do with all this information? How can you make sense of it all and apply it to your own daily life?

To help you continue on your journey, here are a few tips for next steps:

Revisit (or do) the exercises

Each chapter ends with three exercises, designed to help you apply the trait. Take another look at these now and revisit your answers. If you didn't complete the exercises as you were reading the book, now is a good time to work through them. The chapter summary is immediately after them, so you can refresh your memory on the topic at the same time.

Find out more about the winning examples I've shared

I have given you a whole range of different, inspiring people to illustrate the seven traits. From entrepreneurs to politicians, sportspeople to influencers, there may be some who have sparked your interest. Do some more research into those who attract you, to find out what else you can learn from them. Ask yourself why they are of particular interest to you.

Explore the teachers that I've mentioned and see how they might help you

The Mental Boxing™ method and the seven traits I've developed have been significantly influenced by the experts I've featured in each chapter. There is a wealth of additional information on each of them on the internet, plus most have books or courses to help you go deeper. Do your own research and see if there is more you can learn from them to help you in your own transformation.

Arrange a call with me

I'm always willing to speak to anyone who is genuinely curious about Mental Boxing, the seven winning traits and the programmes I offer. Below is a link for you to make a booking.

How To Be a Winner – the seven traits revisited

Reaching our full potential comes from recognising, exploring and studying the daily mental boxing match we all have with ourselves and see how this can sometimes limit us. Here again are the seven traits we can all choose to adopt, so we can enter the boxing ring of life, and business, ready to take on and win the challenges that lie ahead.

Be aware of the choices that you're making

Notice the unconscious programmes you run and how they take you off track. Choose to think differently.

WIN OR LOSE – YOU CHOOSE

Have the courage to take a risk

Take calculated risks with a willingness to face possible failure.

KO FEAR

Never give up

Even if you don't get what you want first second or third time round, keep focussed on what is truly important to you.

FIGHT FOR WHAT YOU WANT

Focus on the future, not the past

Don't base your decisions on past results but on the future you want to create

ROLL WITH THE PUNCHES

Be resilient in all areas of your life

Some of the challenges we face are in our control while others aren't. Either way, acknowledge them, learn and move on.

TAKE IT ON THE CHIN

Be willing to look at things differently

If things aren't working, always be adaptable and seek out new ways to win.

JAB AND MOVE

Be responsible for who you are – own your life

Don't be the victim of your situation or circumstances. Regain your power.

BOXCLEVER

The most important thing to remember about these traits is that they all interconnect. At any moment in your life, you might need to apply two, three or more of the traits to give you the clarity and direction you need.

OTHER RESOURCES FROM BILLY SCHWER

Man Up – The World Champion Way

Boxing is a great metaphor for life. Boxing is commonly known as the noble art, the sweet science, and mastering Billy's 12-round Mental Boxing experience will give you the tools to be more effective, win more often and experience more success.

Intended to support the transformation of the middle-aged man, this book will help them become the champion of their world.

- Knock out negative thoughts, feelings and emotions

- Fight uncertainty and insecurity with power and confidence

- Develop your personal skills to become more effective

- Master the twelve rounds to unleash your potential

- Become a winner in life and in business

Published by Rethink Press

ISBN: 978-1-78133-302-0

Seven Week Group Programme

This group coaching programme is designed for anyone who wants to master the seven winning traits covered in this book.

It includes a live online session each week, a private WhatsApp group, worksheets and an in-depth exploration of each trait and what it means for you.

Become the winner of your life, your work and your world.

To see if this is a good fit for you book a personal call with me:

billyschwer.com/personal-call

Free training

Take my free training course to show you:

- Three critical mistakes made by people... so you can avoid them and live with passion, power and purpose.
- My 3D success model … which has helped people raise their game in health, wealth and relationships
- The seven step winning formula to supercharge your transformation… giving you everything you need to live a 10 out of 10 life.

billyschwer.com/training

Follow me on LinkedIn

I'm always happy to connect with people who are eager to learn more. I share regular content and this is where you'll be able to find out about live events and webinars.

linkedin.com/in/billy-schwer/

If you want to book me to speak

For enquiries about keynote speaking and workshops within your organisation, visit billyschwer.com/keynote for information and to make an enquiry.

HOW TO BE A WINNER